Yesterday's Wirral

D1245797

PORT SUNLIGHT
A Pictorial History
1888 to 1953

INTRODUCTION

Due to the success of our recent publication *Yesterday's Wirral Pictorial History* we have taken the same format and applied it to Port Sunlight. This time we have teamed up with Gavin Hunter, who was an ideal partner having worked at Port Sunlight for 27 years and recently took a Master's Degree in Landscape History, using Lever's impact on Wirral as his specialist subject. Gavin has set the scene on page three for 'The Road to Port Sunlight' and then the book takes us from 'the cutting of the first sod' in 1888 through to the Coronation year of 1953. We have used almost 500 photographs and graphics, many of which came from *Progress* and *Port Sunlight News*, the Lever Brothers' 'in-house' magazines which are a fund of useful information about what was happening in and around the Port Sunlight Village and Lever Brothers' Factory during this period. As with our other publications, the vast majority of these photographs have not been used before in the public domain and we have taken the opportunity to include lots of new pictures and information relating to the people who lived, worked and played in and around Port Sunlight.

Design & origination: Ian Boumphrey

Published by: Ian & Marilyn Boumphrey
The Nook 7 Acrefield Road Prenton
Wirral CH42 8LD
Tel/Fax: 0151 608 7611 e-mail: ian@yesterdayswirral.co.uk
Website: www.yesterdayswirral.co.uk

Printed by: Printfine Ltd Gibraltar Row
Liverpool L3 7HJ Tel: 0151 242 0000
Website: www.printfine.co.uk

ISBN: 1-899241 18 3

**Price
£9.95**

The Road To Port Sunlight
. . . Before 1888

From the foundation of Port Sunlight in 1888 until the accession of Queen Elizabeth II in 1953, six monarchs occupied the British throne. With the notable exception of Victoria, most visited Port Sunlight and all are commemorated in some way in the factory or village. Our history follows the development of this remarkable community from its inception until 1953, some 100 years after the birth of William Hesketh Lever, its founder.

William Lever was born in 1851 into a middle class Bolton family. His father, James Lever, was a wholesale grocery supplier. There were ten children in all – eight girls and the two boys, William Hesketh and his brother James Darcy who together later formed Lever Brothers. They were all brought up in a relatively small terraced house in the centre of Bolton in a narrow cobbled street called Wood Street. The house is still there today, displaying its blue heritage plaque commemorating the fact that it was Lever's birthplace, and the names are commemorated in the first roads built in Port Sunlight – Wood Street and Bolton Road.

William attended a small private school in Wood Street, where at the tender age of six he met the girl who was later to become his wife – Elizabeth Ellen Hulme. He also met his life-long friend Jonathan Simpson who later qualified as an architect and designed several of the houses in Port Sunlight. Both William and Jonathan went on to the local Grammar School but Lever left at the age of 15 to work for his father. In 1882, at the age of twenty-one he became a partner in the family business, and in April 1874 he married his childhood sweetheart at St George's Road Congregational Church, in Bolton. By 1884, when he was only 33 and already a successful businessman, William Lever considered retiring to a remote Scottish island. Instead he became fired with the idea of marketing a product of his own. This was the industrial age when cleanliness was considered almost next to godliness. Lever's simple idea was to take soap, which until then had generally been sold by weight cut into crude blocks and wrapped in newspaper, and to turn it into a branded product, easily recognisable in its own right. He would buy soap, stamped with his own brand name and put it into brightly coloured cartons. Then supported by an extensive advertising campaign of such quality and creativity that even today it still evokes admiration, he would set about selling it to every housewife in the country. Such was its success that, together with his brother James Darcy, they decided to manufacture soap themselves and formed Lever Brothers. They rented a factory in Warrington where, not only could they make their own products, but they could control the quality of the soap they manufactured and sold. Within three years demand had risen so much that, unable to expand and increase production on the Warrington site, they began looking for somewhere else to build their own factory - eventually settling upon the site we know today as…….

Port Sunlight

Elizabeth Ellen Lever
wife of William Lever
1850–1913

William Hesketh Lever
The 1st Lord Leverhulme
1851–1925

James Darcy Lever
William Lever's Brother
1854–1910

Part of the original soap works
at Warrington

James Lever, father of
William and James Lever
1809–1897

Mar 3 — Ceremonial cutting of the first sod to mark the start of the Port Sunlight factory by Mrs Lever

Mar 25 — Birth of William Hulme Lever, only son of Mr & Mrs William Hesketh Lever

Sep — Mr Lever's first visit to America and Canada – a trip of some 15,000 miles with his brother-in-law WF Tillotson

Dec — Construction of houses in Port Sunlight village started

Dec 7 — Registration of 'Lifebuoy' trade mark by Lever Brothers [Sunlight having already been registered on 2 February 1884]

— Mr Lever with his wife and newborn son moved into Thornton Manor (which they rented from the Forwood family)

— Mr Lever's first business trip to Europe

Above: William Owen, Mr Lever's architect from Warrington, who helped him to find the new site for the Port Sunlight factory and village and was responsible for preparing the first plans for their development

Right: Having outgrown the Warrington site William Lever, assisted by his architect William Owen, set about finding a new site to build his factory. After examining various possibilities on both sides of the River Mersey, they eventually settled on an area of marshy farmland criss-crossed by tidal creeks lying between the New Chester Road and the main railway line from Birkenhead to Chester. Nearby Prices Candle Works, established in 1853, had already recognised the potential of this navigable tidal inlet which lay just outside the jurisdiction of the Mersey Docks and Harbour Board. It was here on the 3rd of March 1888 that an invited party of guests came ashore at the 'Stone Quay' to perform the ceremonial cutting of the first sod. They had travelled from Liverpool to New Ferry Pier on the steamer Firefly where they transferred to the steam barge Warrington, 'which was made to have a smart appearance by a covering of crimson cloth', for the final trip to the site

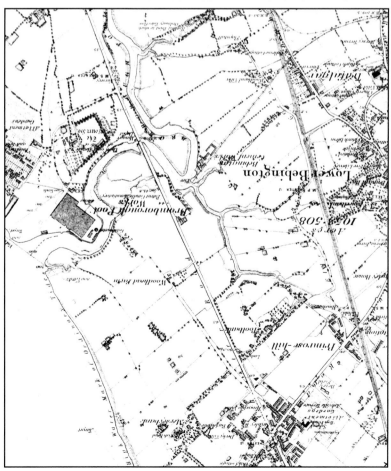

Above: After the ceremony, some 150 guests returned to Liverpool where a banquet to celebrate the event was held in the Bear's Paw Restaurant on Lord Street[PRG]

"Presented to Mrs. W. H. Lever by Messrs. Lever Bros. On the occasion of her cutting the first sod of their new works at Port Sunlight, March 3 1888"

Above: The ceremonial silver spade used by Mrs Lever to start the work on the Port Sunlight factory. Just three weeks later she gave birth to their only son William Hulme Lever who in 1925 became the 2nd Viscount Leverhulme

Above: When work began on the Port Sunlight factory, part of the site was already occupied by the Bebington Cement Works and crossed by the Storeton Quarry Tramway. These two pictures show the 'Stone Quay' where quarry stone was loaded onto barges for shipment to sites elsewhere in the UK and around the world. In the background is New Chester Road

Above: This picture, probably taken somewhere on the shore near to the New Ferry Pier, purports to show some of the guests who attended the ceremony of cutting the first sod. (Port Sunlight News, March 1965)[UN]

Jun 25 First production of *Sunlight* soap commenced at the new Port Sunlight factory

Nov 18 First Printing Department opened in one of the first buildings on Wood Street Port Sunlight (*see photo*)

—   This year was almost entirely devoted to completing the No.1 Factory and getting production started

Above & Left: *Seen from slightly different angles, construction is well underway on the first buildings for Port Sunlight. On the left is the No.1 Soapery. On the right the Glycerine building and in the centre the chimney - eventually reaching a height of over 300ft. Piles of newly-mown hay can still be seen in the fields surrounding the new buildings*

Right: *Seen here from Bromborough Pool No.1 Soapery is still under construction. The building on the left is the Glycerine building. At the corner of the tower rising on the right is the spot where Mrs Lever ceremonially started work on the factory in March 1888*[PRG]

Left: *The same view from Bromborough Pool as the above picture after completion of the No.1 Soapery and packing room. Bromborough Pool gave direct access to the River Mersey for barges bringing materials and products to and from the Port Sunlight factory. On the left is the site where Port Sunlight Dock was constructed*[PRG]

Above: *An early view inside No.1 Soapery showing the riveted soap pans where the oils and fats were boiled with caustic to produce raw soap and glycerine*

Left: *Girls packing soap by hand in the early days of production at Port Sunlight*[PRG]

Right: *The original Printing Department on Wood Street*

May 27   Lever Brothers Ltd registered as a Private Limited Company (with a capital of £300,000 divided into 15,000 preference shares of £10 each and 15,000 ordinary shares of £10 each). William Lever, his brother James Darcy Lever, his father James Lever, and PJ Winser, the Works Manager, were the first directors of the new company

Aug 23   Employees' excursion to Beaumaris, Anglesey on the steamer *Mona's Isle* (*see invitation on this page*)

—   Mr Lever's 2nd trip to America and Canada
—   First Port Sunlight Savings Bank opened
—   The Port Sunlight Brass Band was formed
—   First cottages completed: Nos 1-21 and 14-18 Bolton Road [which were later destroyed by enemy bombing in November 1941]

Above: *Invitation to Beaumaris to celebrate completion of the Port Sunlight works*[PRG]

Above: *The steam boat* Mona's Isle *which conveyed the Lever Brothers employees to Beaumaris on 23 August 1890*

Above: *Lever Brothers employees seen here with Mr & Mrs Lever on their trip to Beaumaris – a somewhat belated celebration of the first production at Port Sunlight*

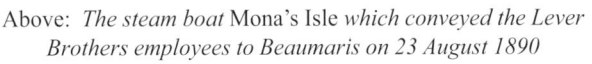

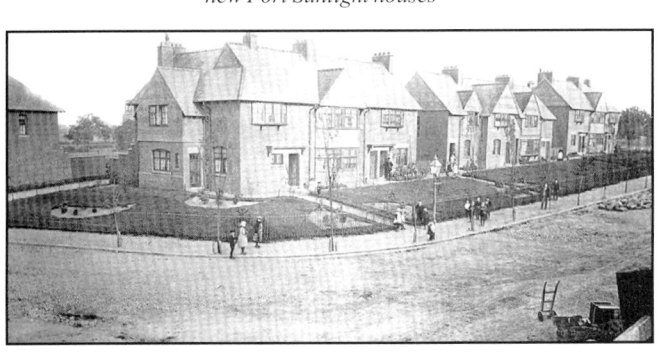

Above: *When Lever began building Port Sunlight, Ellens Lane wound its way between the fields to Bebington Station. This little cottage which stood on Ellens Lane was purchased by Lever and apparently disappeared with the construction of Greendale Road and the new Port Sunlight houses*[PRG]

Left: *Finished soon after the cottages pictured above, these were the first houses in Greendale Road. In the distance on the extreme right was the lamplighter's cottage standing near to where the station is today*

Above: *Photographed from the railway bridge, this view shows the first houses completed in the village. Bolton Road stretches into the distance, still separated from the New Chester Road by a tidal creek. To the right runs Greendale Road, seen in the picture to the left*

Feb 28   Saddle tank locomotive *Sunlight* purchased for use around the Port Sunlight factory

Apr 2   First sale of Lever's *Glycerine*

Aug 15   Works holiday and Garden Fete at *Thornton Manor* with some 5,000 employees and their families present

Nov 28   Gladstone Hall opened by the Rt Hon WE Gladstone (*see photos*)

Nov 30   Mr & Mrs Lever left for a 6 week holiday to the South of France & Egypt

—   The Village shop opened – later to become Port Sunlight's Post Office (*see photo*)

—   First Souvenir Brochure of Port Sunlight village issued

—   Houses completed: 2-12 Bolton Road; 71-87 Greendale Road & No.88, the Post Office

Above: *This is the first shop in Port Sunlight opened in 1891. Standing on the corner of Greendale Road and Park Road it became the Post Office when the new shops opened on Bridge Street in 1894*

Left: *This is the exterior view of Gladstone Hall which opened on 28 November 1891. In the background stands* Woodland Villa, *later demolished to make way for Lever's main offices*

Below: *Interior view of Gladstone Hall with benches and tables. During the day it served as the Men's Dining Hall. In the evening it was used as a village hall, and on Sundays for religious concerts*[PRG]

Above left: *Sketch taken from* The Illustrated London News *of Rt Hon WE Gladstone addressing the audience after he officially opened Gladstone Hall in 1891*

Left: *The names of first three locomotives purchased by Lever Brothers can be seen on the side of the engines and were from left to right:-* Sunlight (1891), Progress (1900) *and* Sydney (1896)[PRG]

Below: *Barges being loaded with cases of soap at the Port Sunlight wharf. The tidal inlet at the mouth of the River Dibbin enabled them to shuttle to and from sea-going vessels in the River Mersey and at the nearby ports of Birkenhead and Liverpool*

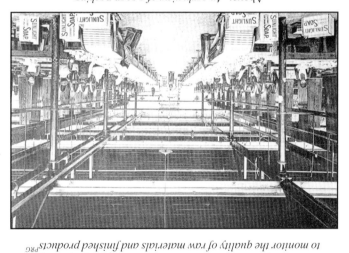

Above: *An early view of a soap packing room. Slatted timber conveyors moved the wooden soap boxes along the room as the girls filled them with stamped soap tablets*

Above: *One of the original laboratories at Port Sunlight factory, used to monitor the quality of raw materials and finished products* PSC

Jan 14	Mr & Mrs Lever return from their 6-week visit to France & Egypt
Jan 28	Port Sunlight Village Council formed
Feb 8	Mr Lever elected Chairman of the Liberal Executive Committee of Bebington & New Ferry District
May 7	Mrs Lever crowned the May Queen at Charles Thompson Mission in Birkenhead whilst Mr Lever gave the address
Jun 9	Port Sunlight AFC were one of the founder members of the West Cheshire Association Football League
Jun 11	Lever Brothers appointed Soap Makers to HM Queen Victoria
Jul 4	William Lever stood as Liberal candidate for Birkenhead in the General Election – defeated by Lord Bury (Conservative) by 604 votes
Jul 22	One-day strike of Stamping Room girls and boys in support of demand for four shillings a month bonus
Aug 6	Annual Port Sunlight Fete & Sports held at *Thornton Manor* attended by some 7,000 people
Sep	Mr & Mrs Lever, accompanied by their 4-year-old son William Hulme Lever, started their round-the-world voyage aboard the White Star Liner *Germanic*
—	The Sick, Funeral and Medical Aid Society formed. In return for weekly payments of between 2d and 8d, members and their families were entitled to free medical attendance. Sick benefits varied from 2 shillings & six pence to 10 shillings per week and funeral benefits from £1 to £8
—	Houses built: 9-15 Wood Street

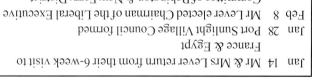

Mar 9	Mr & Mrs Lever and their son return from their round-the-world trip
Apr 18	Completion of the sale of *Thornton Manor*, which they had previously rented, to Mr & Mrs Lever (*see photo*)
Jul 22	Some 2,400 women & children went to Blackpool in 4 trains for the Lever Brothers Staff Excursion
Oct 30	Registration of the *Vim* trade mark by Lever Brothers Ltd
Nov 28	Eliza Lever – William Hesketh Lever's mother died in Bolton
—	Soap-making capacity increased by the first extension to No1 Soapery
—	There were no houses completed in 1893

Above: *William Lever (seated centre with hat) seen here with a party of visiting wholesale grocers from the Manchester District in front of No.1 Soapery prior to its extension in 1893*[PRG]

Left: *This is how Thornton Manor, home of Mr & Mrs Lever, appeared in 1893 when they finally bought the property which until then they had rented from the Forwood family. Very soon alterations started to replace the gables and bays (creating the house as it appears on page15)*

Left: *Standing immediately opposite the new extensions to the No.1 factory, these cottages are Nos. 18-22 Bridge Street. It took its name from the arched sandstone bridge which spans the centre of the Dell Park and divides the two halves of Bridge Street*

Below: *From the earliest days of Port Sunlight, allotments have been a fundamental part of the lives of villagers, being seen as a healthy relief for people confined to the factory all day, as well as supplementing the family diet*[PRG]

By 1893, building around the west end of the Dell Park, the only remains of the former tidal creeks still visible in the village today, was gaining momentum and the first houses on Park Road and Bridge Street were ready for occupation the following year

Left: *Park Road which lies on either side of the Dell Park was amongst the first roads to be completed in the village. Seen here two ladies are walking in front of No.10 Park Road with No.2 on the right*

Right: *The Employees' Provident Society Store pictured on the right which was better known as 'The Store' was opened 26 April 1894 and stood on the corner of Bridge Street and Bolton Road. As the title suggests it was controlled and financed by employees with no control from the Company. Each member had to hold at least £2 worth of shares which could be paid off at 3d per week. Besides selling grocery products, The Store also sold drapery, boots, ready-made clothing, coal, confectionery etc [later the home of Mac Fisheries, it was destroyed by enemy action in March 1941 and was never rebuilt]*PRC

Left: Lifebuoy Household SoapUNI was first offered for sale on 9 April 1894

Jan 16	First sale of double refined *Glycerine*
Apr 9	First sale of *Lifebuoy Household Soap*
Jun 21	Lever Brothers Limited incorporated as a Public Liability Company
Jul	Eight-hour working day introduced – one of the first companies in the country to do so – the Stonemasons of Birkenhead present a tablet to mark the occasion
Jul 7	Company excursion to Llandudno
Aug 25	The Port Sunlight Horticultural Society held its first show - 25 entrants of whom 21 won prizes
Oct	Mr Lever visited USA and Canada, sailing on the *Lucania* – accompanied by his 2 sisters
Oct 17	William Lever stood as Liberal candidate for Birkenhead in the by-election – defeated by Elliott Lees (Conservative) with majority of 106
Dec	Of the 54 allotments in the village, 18 were in Greendale Road but the 28 in Bolton Road had to move when the land was built on
Dec 14	The recently established Girls' Social Club met for its first social evening in Gladstone Hall
—	The Dell Bridge was built. It included a vertical sundial carved into the outside of the sandstone parapet (*see photo*)
—	The Village shop on the corner of Park Road and Greendale Road became the Post Office
—	Three shops were opened to run on co-operative lines - on the corner of Bridge Street & Bolton Road [later destroyed in World War II]
—	*Bridge Cottage* was built. (Mr Lever lived here 1896/7 with his family whilst building work was carried out at *Thornton Manor*). No.23 Park Road, it is now the home of the Minister of Christ Church
—	Houses built: 1-9 & 2-22 Bridge Street; 89-92 Greendale Road; 1-23, 2-24 & 28-36 Park Road; and 1-7 & 17-25 Wood Street

Above: *The Cottages pictured are 7-9 Bridge Street. Surrounded here by bushes, trees and iron railings which disappeared in the 1940s, they look very different from the scene today*

Above: *The Dell Bridge, spanning the former tidal creek which had been drained and turned into a park, was opened in 1894. the vertical sundial, carved on the outside of the parapet, can be seen here above the arch*

Above: *Looking out across the Dell Park, these houses stand on the corner of Park Road and Bridge Street. On the left is No.26 Park Road, in the centre No.1 Bridge Street and next door to the right is No.3*

Right: *Port Sunlight Dock was opened on 2 July 1895. With its massive timber lock gates across the entrance it enabled larger sea-going vessels to tie up right alongside the factory during high tide*

Above: *No.28 Park Road was completed in 1895 was designed by William Owen, Lever's original architect of the Port Sunlight factory, who was responsible for a large number of the houses in Park Road*

Above: *No.50 Park Road, completed in 1895 and known locally as Swiss Cottage was amongst the second phase of housing to be built on Park Road. It was designed by the architects Grayson & Ould who were also responsible for the Bridge Inn and Co-Partners Club*

Corner: 1-8 Riverside and 27-55 Wood Street

— Houses completed: 38-52 Park Road; 2-8 Poets

— Port Sunlight AFC West Cheshire AF League Champions 1894/95

— The first Port Sunlight Cycling Club was founded

— Illness prevents James Darcy Lever (the 'other' brother to William Hesketh Lever in Lever Brothers) taking any further active part in the business

— *Port Sunlight Monthly Journal* was introduced

— First publication of the *Sunlight Year Book* and *Sunlight Almanac* which was given free to users of *Sunlight Soap* on the purchase of 12 tablets of soap

Feb   Soap-making capacity increased to 1,600 tons a week

Feb 18   Port Sunlight Branch of the British Women's Temperance Society was founded. Over 300 girls sat down to a tea provided by Mrs Lever

Mar 7   First Annual General Meeting of Lever Brothers Limited held at the *City Terminus Hotel*, London

Mar 13   Mr & Mrs Lever sailed on SS *Majestic* for America with their 7-year-old son, together with their nephew and niece

Apr 23   The newly formed Port Sunlight Village Council approved an application from the Cricket Club to have their field mowed, rolled and 'put in order'

Apr 30   Port Sunlight AFC were declared winners of the Wirral League Cup 1894/95

May 11   Official opening of the Greendale Road Bowling Green with the Sunlight Brass Band in attendance

May 29   Mr & Mrs Lever and family returned from America

Jun   An article in the June 1895 edition of the *Port Sunlight Monthly Journal* was entitled: "Proposed Decimal Coinage in the United Kingdom"

Jul 2   Port Sunlight Dock opened (*see photo*)

Jul 13   The employees' excursion to Blackpool attracted some 2,900 adults and 760 children

Jul 18   At the Village Council meeting it was agreed to allow the Football Club expenses incurred for refreshments at official club fixtures ie sherry and lemonade [but no mention if they were supplied before, during or after matches!].
The Grounds Committee complained of pigeons, fowls and dogs trespassing on the allotments - it was suggested a notice be sent to the owners of these animals - one member suggested the allotments should be let out for shooting

Jul 16   William Lever stood again at the General Election as Liberal Candidate for Birkenhead – lost by 204 votes

Aug 3   Second Annual Port Sunlight Floral and Horticultural Show held in the Gladstone Hall - the Port Sunlight Band was in attendance - admission 6d, but free to employees and their families

Sep 21   Mr Lever and family left for business trip to South Africa and Australia aboard the *Tantallon Castle*

Oct 15   Formation of the Port Sunlight Gymnasium Club using a room in new buildings adjoining the railway

Nov   The Port Sunlight Chess Club was formed

Dec 17   The Grounds Committee reported that some employees were taking a short cut through the allotments and then over the temporary bridge to the New Chester Road

1896

Apr — It was proposed to establish a Volunteer Corps at Port Sunlight but only 19 names were forthcoming when over 60 were required

May — All the cricket matches for the coming season were cancelled as the ground was totally unfit

May 2 — Construction of No.2 Soapery started

Jun 13 — The Port Sunlight Prize Band were awarded first prize at a contest in Birkenhead against 8 other bands from Lancashire & Cheshire

Jun 27 — The Port Sunlight branch of the British Women's Temperance Society were conveyed to their annual picnic at Raby Mere by waggonettes where splendid weather enhanced their fun and pleasure

Jul 21 — The Village Council reported that they were unable to pay the rent on the New Ferry football field which had increased from £12 to £18

Aug — It was stated that the Port Sunlight Amateur Dramatic Society was threatened with extinction due to lack of enthusiasm

Aug 10 — Park Road Schools opened with 90 infants and 93 seniors (see photo)

Aug 11 — The Co-partners' Club (later the Mens' Club) opened – colloquially known as 'The Pavilion'

Sep — The Port Sunlight AFC entered the Liverpool & Wirral and District League

Sep 1 — Girls' Hostel erected (later to become the Library/ Museum/Bank and then the Heritage Centre) included a restaurant where a good meal could be purchased for 3d

Oct — The Village Council decided that control of the Gymnasium Buildings (which also contained the Fire Brigade Appliances) should be vested in the Athletic Committee

Oct — The Vicar of Rock Ferry asked permission to use the large School Hall once a month for a Church of England service. This was refused by the Village Council for the time being, with a sub-committee appointed to discuss the matter

Nov 14 — Lever Brothers purchased 3 motor vans and decorated them with *Sunlight Soap* adverts. They hit the headlines when a new act came into force allowing horseless vehicles to proceed without a man in front with a red flag (see photo)

Dec — The East Wing and Vestibule of Port Sunlight Offices were completed

Dec 8 — The Girls' Institute (Collegium) opened (above the village shops on the corner of Bridge Street and Bolton Road)

— Mr Lever and his family moved into *Bridge Cottage* during work at *Thornton Manor*

— A replica of Shakespeare's birthplace built at 'Poets Corner' (see photo)

— Saddle tank locomotive *Sydney* purchased for use around the factory. The first of three locomotives at Port Sunlight to bear the name *Sydney*

— Houses built: 1 Bath Street; 20-42 Bolton Road 1-9 Cross Street, 1-3 Poets Corner (Shakespeare's Cottages)

Above: This interior view was taken at Park Road Schools which opened on 10 August 1896 with 90 infants and 93 seniors. In 1903 the schools moved to Church Drive and the Park Road Schools later became a Management Training Centre PRG

Above: This replica of Shakespeare's birthplace was built in 1896 at 'Poets Corner' and was demolished in December 1938

Above: In 1896 Lever Brothers purchased 3 motor vans and decorated them with Sunlight Soap[UNI] adverts following a new Motor Car Act which allowed a horseless vehicle to proceed without a man in front carrying a red flag - the vans were to take part in the first London to Brighton motor-car run which was to set off at 10.30am on 14 November 1886. However, Mr Lever stole a march on all the other 54 vehicles by starting off at midnight (when the new Act came into force). The vans set off in procession from the Metropole Hotel in London, causing a great deal of interest - the Daily Mail carried an article entitled "Sunlight at Midnight"

Jan — Now 238 houses completed in the village, occupied by 878 persons

Jan 26 — The Port Sunlight Allotments Committee asked that allotment holders should put at least one load of manure on their plot annually

Jan 29 — Soap-making capacity increased to 2,400 tons per week

Apr — Port Sunlight Bowling Club groundsman appointed

Apr 7 — Construction of the Cotton Seed Oil and Cake Mills started

Apr 28 — The Co-operative Stores opened for the sale of grocery and provisions with stock transferred from the old shop which was vacated to become the Post Office

May — The poor children of the Hemingford Street Mission, Birkenhead (later Charles Thompson Mission) were entertained at Gladstone Hall

May 3 — Grounds Committee reported there were 89 allotments at the beginning of the year. Several had been lost to the new bridge and road, and 2 lost when flooded by the tide. However, 16 new plots were added making a total of 100

May 3 — The Recreation Ground in front of the Girls' Institute was declared ready [originally] tennis courts, now Bolton Road Bowling Green] The Lawn Tennis and Croquet Club was founded — several gentlemen desired to join the Tennis Club but could only be admitted subject to the approval of the Village Council

May 26 — Death of James Lever aged 87 at Thornton Hough — (father of the brothers William Hesketh & James Darcy Lever)

May 29 — Funeral of Mr James Lever who was buried at All Saints' Church Thornton Hough

Jun 26 — Port Sunlight Schools had a 'Royal Treat' to commemorate Queen Victoria's Diamond Jubilee — two large fields had been prepared for the various entertainments with Mr & Mrs Lever in attendance — this was followed by tea in Gladstone Hall

Jul 3 — Six trains transported some 2,300 employees of Lever Bros from Birkenhead to London where they enjoyed a day in the capital where their mode of transport was either a wagonette or specially chartered omnibus. The trip included a visit to the Earl's Court Exhibition to celebrate Queen Victoria's Diamond Jubilee

Jul 20 — The Village Council Meeting agreed to the formation

of the Port Sunlight Photographic Society

Jul 21 — Victoria Bridge opened by the Premier of New South Wales (see photos opposite)

Aug — It was stated that the Port Sunlight Amateur Dramatic Society was once again threatened with extinction due to lack of enthusiasm

Aug — The Port Sunlight Photographic Society was formed

Aug — Mr WH Lever visited Switzerland with his wife and son

Sep 21 — The Village Council decided there should be no football club formed this season

Oct 10 — First Sunday Morning Services held in the village (in Park Road Schools)

Oct 12 — First toilet soap made at Port Sunlight

Dec — A series of cinematographic views were shown to the children of Port Sunlight Schools - one of the first showings of moving pictures in this country

— Lever Brothers were one of the first companies to use moving pictures for advertising purposes

— William Owen, Lever's first architect, made a director of the company

— Houses built: 3-33 Bath Street and 9-10 Riverside

Below: Nos. 9-31 Bath Street, which were built in 1897, pictured here a few years later

Above: The original tennis courts on Bolton Road, now occupied by the bowling green

Left: Mr Lever at the reigns of his carriage outside Bridge Cottage where he and his family lived whilst major alteration work was being carried out at their home at Thornton Manor

Left: Reflected in the waters of the tidal creek, Victoria Bridge seen here under construction.PRG

Below is part of an account of the opening of Victoria Bridge described in the Port Sunlight Monthly Journal in August 1897:-

"The bridge is in one arch of masonry of 100 feet clear span with a rise of 12.5 feet, being a segment of a circle with a radius of 107 feet. It has a total length of 187 feet along its parapets.... The masonry is of Anglesey limestone, whilst the cores of the abutments are of solid cement concrete....

The parapets are also of limestone masonry, panelled and surmounted with a coping, and it is on the inside of the parapets at the centre that the bridge has its name and date inscribed: "Victoria Bridge, 1897." These parapets widen out at each end to 40 feet, so as to meet the Bolton-road....

The bridge has been erected in less than twelve months by Messrs. Lever Brothers' own staff, from the designs and under the superintendence of the architect, Mr. Wm. Owen, F.R.I.B.A., of Warrington. The total weight of the bridge, including the earth embankment, is 26,000 tons, of which over 9,000 tons are solid masonry and concrete.

By noon on Wednesday, July 21st the platforms on each side of the New Chester Road end of the bridge were beginning to fill. Mr. Owen, the architect, and his wife appeared on the scene. By-and-by came the Mayor with the Mayoress....

Across the roadway of the bridge stretched a cord tied in the middle with ribbons red, white, and blue. Till at once we saw a procession walking over from the other side of the bridge, the Honourable George H. Reid leading the way with Mrs. Lever, followed by Mr. Lever, Mr. and Mrs. Winser, Mr. and Mrs. Ferguson, Master Willie Lever, and others. Then the ceremony began....

Mr. Owen presented the cord wherewith the silver scissors was to be cut. Mr. Reid, before applying them, told us how glad he was to come to a place that fell so like home, and was so beautiful. Then he gave the magic cut and named the "Victoria Bridge," and our band struck up "God save the Queen." After the photographers had "taken" us as we stood, we proceeded informally up Bolton Road, and round the Park to the Gladstone Hall."

Above: The fisherman is taking advantage of the creek which was spanned by Victoria Bridge. This handsome structure was buried when the creek was filled in – (see account on this page.)

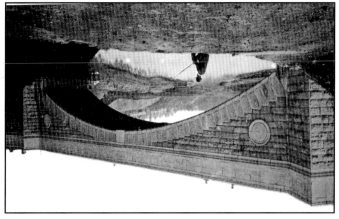

Above: This was the scene when the Rt Hon George H Reid, Premier of New South Wales, Australia, officially opened Victoria Bridge (named after Queen Victoria in her Jubilee year) by cutting the ribbon with silver scissors on 21 July 1897. In the centre of the signatories is Mr Lever, and on their right in the cap his 11 year-old son, William Hulme Lever.
The bridge spanned the tidal creek which ran across the line of Bolton Road enabling it to be linked for traffic to the New Chester Road (see picture below right).
This was described as a 'red letter' day for Port Sunlight with the village being decorated with Venetian masts, festoons, flags etc. The creek was eventually filled in and the handsome arch buried, although the roadway is still being used. The parapets were removed and re-used on the New Chester Road Bridge under which the railway line to Planters passed, whilst the date stones have recently been placed in the flower bed opposite the Bridge Inn which was later named after the bridge it stood alongside (see page 19)PRG

Above: Laying the roadway on Victoria Bridge

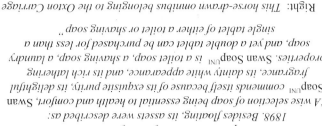

Right: *This horse-drawn omnibus belonging to the Oxton Carriage Co. is seen outside houses in New Chester Road on the New Ferry – Bromborough route. George Davies, one of the original Port Sunlight photographers, lived in the end house on the left*

Above: *Swan Soap*[UNI] *went on sale for the first time on 27 October 1898. Besides floating, its assets were described as:*

"A wise selection of soap being essential to health and comfort, Swan Soap[UNI] *commends itself because of its exquisite purity, its delightful fragrance, its dainty white appearance, and its rich lathering properties. Swan Soap*[UNI] *is a toilet soap, a shaving soap, a laundry soap, and yet a double tablet can be purchased for less than a single tablet of either a toilet or shaving soap."*

Above: *This bird's-eye view of Port Sunlight shows it in relation to the River Mersey, with Birkenhead in the distance on the left. Liverpool is on the right and New Brighton Tower in the centre distance*

Below: *The same buildings as above, with the railway embankment in the foreground, but this view correctly does not include the second phase of No.2 Soapery, which wasn't completed until 1900*

Above: *The taller buildings on the right housed the original Park Road Schools which were opened in the summer of 1896, accommodated 500 children. Due to the then ever-expanding village the schools were enlarged with the lower buildings on the left, opening in 1898*

Although these two artist-drawn views of Port Sunlight both date from 1898 they differ slightly

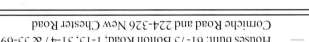

— Corniche Road and 224-326 New Chester Road
— Houses built: 61-75 Bolton Road; 1-15, 31-47 & 55-69
— Park Road Schools enlarged
  (*see photo opposite*)
— Completion of first alterations to *Thornton Manor*

Oct 27 First sale of *Swan* soap (*see photo*)

Jul 4 United States & Canadian grocers visit Port Sunlight

May 16 Authorised capital of Lever Brothers Ltd increased from £2,000,000 to £3,000,000

Apr 17 First Sunday School opened in Park Road Schools

Mar 25 First sale of *Sunlight Cattle Seed Cake*

Mar 21 First sale of Toilet Soap

Mar Last issue of the *Port Sunlight Monthly Journal*

Feb 18 James Darcy Lever officially retired from Lever Brothers due to ill health

Jan 3 Book Binding Department opened at Port Sunlight

Jan Mr Lever visited Switzerland again

Above: *An early view of Port Sunlight Dock with vessels moored opposite the Cotton Seed Oil and Cake Mills*

Above: *The New Chester Road predates the building of Port Sunlight by some 60 years. Built by Thomas Brassey as a turnpike to speed the coaches between Tranmere and Bromborough, the toll-bar stood in nearby New Ferry – the houses seen here are 294-300 New Chester Road and were built in 1898*

Above: *The children are playing in front of Nos.55-59 Corniche Road which derived its name from the fact it lay alongside the deep ravine where the tidal creek ran through the village after passing under Victoria Bridge*

Above: *Thornton Manor, home of Mr Lever and his family, seen here after completion of the first alterations. The square bays have been replaced with semi-circular bays and Dutch gables have been introduced. (This house was eventually incorporated into Thornton Manor as we see it today following the extensive alterations of 1913 & 1914)*

Below: The Bridge Inn, which took its name from the fact it stood at one end of Victoria Bridge (see 1897), is pictured here during its construction PRC

Jan 18 — The American firm of Benjamin Brook & Co was acquired by Lever Brothers and their *Monkey Brand* scouring powder was then to be manufactured at Port Sunlight (*see photo*)

Mar 21 — Authorised capital of Lever Brothers Ltd increased from £3,000,000 to £3,500,000

Apr — First sale of *Monkey Brand*

Apr 15 — The Silver Wedding Fountain was erected to commemorate Mr & Mrs Lever's 25th wedding anniversary (*see photo*)

Jul 8 — Some 3,500 employees visited Llandudno

Aug 5 — Fifth Annual Exhibition of Port Sunlight Floral & Horticultural Society held in Gladstone Hall

Aug 17 — Fire broke out in the factory at No.2 Wood Box, but due to the prompt action of a fitter, the Fire Brigade was called out and had the fire under control in less than an hour

Oct — First edition of *Progress* - the predecessor of the *Port Sunlight News* (which was edited at Port Sunlight until 1926 before transferring to London)

Nov 2 — First section of the West Wing of the Port Sunlight General Offices completed

Nov 6 — A Patriotic Fund was set up to provide for the dependants of the Reservists who were called out from Port Sunlight for active service in the Boer War

Nov 14 — The Suggestion Bureau and Works Council were started

Nov 14 — Construction of the first section of No.2 Soapery completed and opened

— First Sale of *Sunlight Flakes*

— Mr WH Lever rented a furnished house in Hoylake for the summer

— Houses built: 45-109 Bebington Road; 2-8 Boundary Road; 2-16 & 28-38 Circular Drive; 17-35 & 49-53 Corniche Road; 18-24 & 59-63 Greendale Road; 12-20 Lodge Lane; 128-132, 148-168 & 178-222 New Chester Road; 1-7, 19-25, 41-53 & 69-75 Pool Bank and 2-56, Primrose Hill

Above: The pretty stone semi-circular fountain with seats either end was erected to commemorate Mr & Mrs Lever's 25th wedding anniversary. It was originally sited on Park Road at the end of the Dell opposite the Post Office. It later moved to a position outside the station before finally moving to its present position by the Greendale Road bowling green. It was inscribed:

"Silver Wedding Fountain. W.H. – E.F.L. April 15, 1874. Erected by the employees of Lever Brothers Limited, April 15, 1899, and to the memory of James and Eliza Lever, parents of the founder of Port Sunlight, who wishes here to place on record the fact that Port Sunlight would have been impossible of realization by him without the influence of their example and careful training."

*The American firm of Benjamin Brook & Co was acquired on 18 January 1899 and their Monkey Brand*UNI *scouring powder was then manufactured at Port Sunlight. Advertising contained the celebrated slogan 'won't wash clothes' and the brand was described later by Lever Brothers as:*

"A Wonderful Home Beautifier – With an old towel, a bowl of water, and a bar of *Monkey Brand*, a housewife can work wonders in making home 'the brightest spot on earth'. *Monkey Brand* does its work silently, rapidly and effectively"

Above: *This was the front cover ot the first edition of* Progress[PRG]

Above: *Primrose Hill took its name from the area adjoining Bebington Road which existed before the building of Port Sunlight. These pretty cottages replaced the earlier low quality houses which stood on Primrose Hill. The children are standing outside Nos. 28-40*

Right: *The Cottages pictured in New Chester Road number134-156 and were all constructed in1899*

Below: *This view of the houses on Corniche Road was taken from the dry ravine, known as the Corniche Dell, which resulted from the damming of the tidal creek which passed under Victoria Bridge. Lying to the rear of Christ Church, it has since been filled in and is now occupied by grass and tree-lined footpaths*

Jan		*Sunlight Flakes* relaunched as *Lux Flakes*
Jan	24	Mr & Mrs Lever were 'At Home' at *Thornton Manor* to some 220 employees from Port Sunlight
Jan	27	Meeting of the Port Sunlight Branch of the British Womens' Temperance Association held in the Girl's Institute
Feb	5	The Port Sunlight Amateur Orchestral Society was established
Mar	5	Construction of Hulme Hall commenced
Mar	14	The inaugural meeting of the 1st Port Sunlight Company of the Boys' Brigade was held in the Gladstone Hall
May	25/27	Over 1,600 employees make the 2-day trip to the great Paris Exhibition
May	26	Some 2,000 Sunlighters, mainly juniors, enjoyed a trip to the Isle of Man on the *Monas Queen & Monas Isle* - both paddle steamers were specially chartered for the trip
Jun	15	Port Sunlight Day Schools Annual Summer Treat was a trip for 290 children to New Brighton
Aug	31	Induction at Gladstone Hall of Port Sunlight's first pastor, The Rev Samuel Gamble-Walker
Sep	22	First manufacture of *Lever's Dry Soap* and *Y-Z Royal Disinfectant Soap Powder* (which stood for 'wise head')
Oct		The *Bridge Inn* opened - initially conducted wholly on temperance lines which meant no licence for alcohol until a 6-day licence was granted in 1903 (*see photo opposite*)
Oct	17	Mr Lever stood as Liberal candidate for Birkenhead but was defeated by Joseph Hoult
Oct	25/26	In a 'Polishing Competition' at Christ Church Sale of Work sponsored by *Monkey Brand*, ladies vigorously restored pennies to new-mint brightness to win various prizes
Nov	22	The Girls' Institute had its re-opening night in the Gladstone Hall
Dec	1	Soap-making capacity increased to 3,200 tons per week following the completion of 2nd half of No.2 Soapery

—	Estimated population of Port Sunlight 2,007
—	The Caxton Cycling Club formed in connection with the Printing Department
—	Saddle tank locomotive *Progress* delivered to the factory
—	Houses built: 2-10 Lodge Lane, 134-146 & 170-176 New Chester Road,14-16 Church Drive and 23-27 Windy Bank

Above: *The 1st Port Sunlight Company Boys Brigade are parading outside Gladstone Hall in 1900. The West Wing of the General Offices can be seen in the background*[PRG]

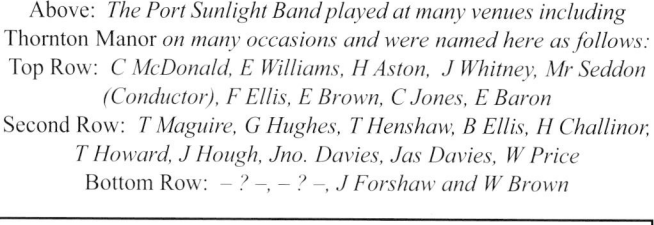

Above: *The Port Sunlight Band played at many venues including Thornton Manor on many occasions and were named here as follows:*
Top Row: *C McDonald, E Williams, H Aston, J Whitney, Mr Seddon (Conductor), F Ellis, E Brown, C Jones, E Baron*
Second Row: *T Maguire, G Hughes, T Henshaw, B Ellis, H Challinor, T Howard, J Hough, Jno. Davies, Jas Davies, W Price*
Bottom Row: *– ? –, – ? –, J Forshaw and W Brown*

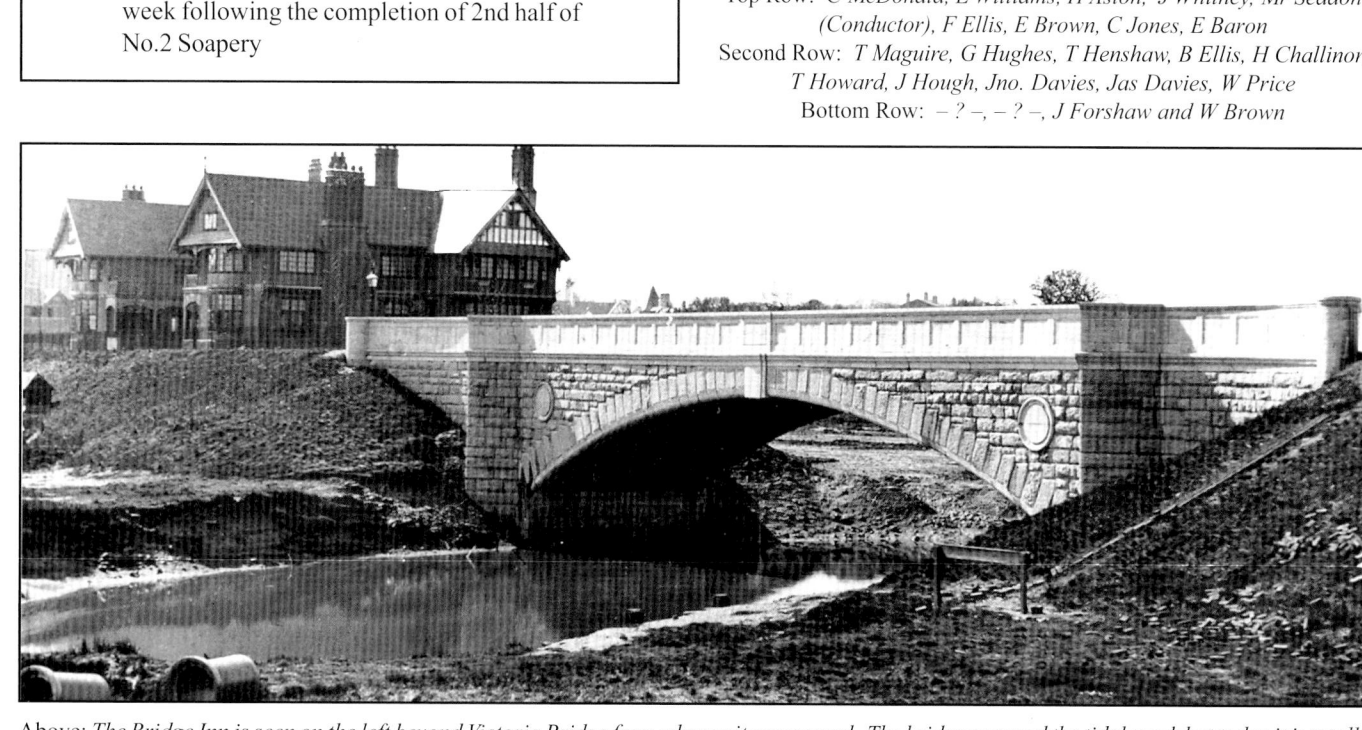

Above: *The Bridge Inn is seen on the left beyond Victoria Bridge from whence it was named. The bridge spanned the tidal creek but today it is totally covered, and buried below the existing roadway. The parapets were removed and used on a nearby railway bridge on the New Chester Road*

Left: This is an early picture of the cobble-stoned Stable Yard behind Gladstone Hall. The Stables and Lodge in the centre originally stood on the site where the West Wing extension to the Main Offices was built in 1899[PRG]

Above: *Rev Samuel Gamble Walker was installed as Port Sunlight's first Pastor on 31 August 1900 at a ceremony in Gladstone Hall. He later went on to become the first Minister of Christ Church*

Above: *The* Bridge Inn *opened in October 1900 and was initially conducted wholly on temperance lines which meant there was no licence for alcohol. This changed following a referendum in the village when a six-day licence was granted in 1903. This licence remaining in force for some 70 years*

Left: *In January of 1900* Sunlight Flakes[UNI] *were relaunched as* Lux Flakes[UNI]

Above: *Some of the 1,600 employees, who made the two-day trip to the great Paris Exhibition on 25/26 May 1900, are pictured waiting for a train on the platform of Bebington Station[PRG]*

Right: *The children are playing in front of houses on the original Ellens Lane. They were designed by Wilson & Talbot and built in 1901. After the redesign of the village in 1910 this became The Causeway (No.18 on the right to No.21 on the left)*

Jan 7	First of 3 receptions for employees held at Thornton Manor
Jan 22	**Queen Victoria died**
Jan 27	Services were held in the schools at Port Sunlight to remember Queen Victoria
Jan 30	Company's first suggestion award given
Mar 2	Memorial Service at Port Sunlight Schools for Queen Victoria
Apr	*Lux* and *Y-Z* were offering high-class photographs of celebrities
Mar 19	Port Sunlight Cycling Club re-formed *(see photo)*
Apr 1	A letter was received from Commander RN Scott, prior to his expedition to the South Pole, thanking Lever Bros for their generous present of one gross (12 dozen) of both *Lifebuoy* and *Sunlight Soaps* and they ordered a further gross of each
Apr 2	Visit to Port Sunlight of the Boer War VC hero Sergeant Richardson of 'The Strathcona's Horse' who was Canadian but had been born in Liverpool
Apr 28	The biggest fire to-date in the Wirral Peninsula destroyed four wood-box sheds at the bottom of Wood Street *(see photos)*
May 18	Registration of *Lux* trademark
Jun	The Village Band were presented with a complete set of new Boosey & Co silver-plated instruments by the Chairman and Directors of Lever Bros
Jun 4	Plans passed for the open-air baths at Port Sunlight
Jun 15	Employees annual excursion when some 4,000 people were transported from New Ferry Stage across to Liverpool Landing Stage where *Monas Isle*, *Queen Victoria* and *Monas Queen* carried them over to the Isle of Man
Jul 27	The 1st Port Sunlight Company of the Boys' Brigade annual camp was held at Ramsey, Isle of Man
Jul 29	Hulme Hall opened as Girls' Dining Room by Mrs Winser, wife of the Works Manager - built at a cost of £20,000 *(see photo)*
Aug 24	Port Sunlight Horticultural Society's Annual Show held at Hulme Hall for the first time
Nov 27	His Royal Highness the Crown Prince of Siam visited Port Sunlight Works and Village
—	Started building a dam to cut off the tidal creeks and allow their filling in *(see 1903)*
—	Port Sunlight Section of the 1st Cheshire Royal Engineers Volunteers formed
—	Mr Lever set out on another round-the-world trip
—	Houses built: 5-10 Brook Street; 1-5 Church Drive; 6-10 & 25-58 Greendale Road; 1-13 Lower Road; 27-39 Pool Bank; 37-45 Primrose Hill and 1-7 & 18-22 The Causeway

Above: An exterior view of Hulme Hall which opened on 29 July at a cost of £20,000. During the day it served as a Girls' Dining Room, during the evenings as a village hall, and was later used to display Mr Lever's collection of antiques and pictures

Above: Three cottages in Greendale Road. From the left No.40-43, built in 1901 and designed by Grayson & Ould

Above: This is an early photograph of the Port Sunlight Cycling Club on what is now the Lever Club Bowling Green, with the Post Office in the background. Note the badges on the front of the member's caps PRG

Above: *The cottage on the right with the children outside is No.30 Greendale Road with No.31 next door and No. 32 beyond. They were all designed by Grayson & Ould and built in 1901. The gardens in front of all the houses in the village were originally surrounded by railings which were taken away in the 1940s*

Above: *These two photographs were taken on 28 April 1901 when the biggest fire up until then in the Wirral Peninsula destroyed four wood-box sheds at the bottom of Wood Street near Poet's Corner. At one stage flames reached 40 ft. into the air but the fire was brought under control within four hours without spreading to other buildings[PRG]*

Above: *The Port Sunlight Village Band was presented by the Chairman and Directors of Lever Brothers Limited with a complete set of silver-plated instruments by Boosey & Co of London. The services were engaged of Mr William Halliwell, the well-known Lancashire Band Instructor to lead the 27 members of the band who were all Lever Brothers Employees[PRG]*

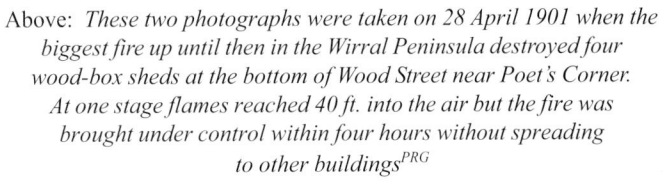

Above: *These cottages in Greendale Road, which were built in 1901, were designed by Ernest George & Yates and number from the left 29-39*

Above: *The cottage with the pointed roof is now No.1 The Causeway on the corner of Greendale Road with Nos. 2-3 to the left. Designed by Grayson & Ould and built in 1901 when the road was originally known as "Ellens Rocks"*

Above: *Work has started on building the Port Sunlight Swimming Pool[PRG]*

Mar	Mr Lever agreed to act as Chairman of the Lower Bebington Urban District Council
Mar 1	First sale of *Velvet Skin* soap
Mar 3	Nurse Crompton started her duties as the newly appointed Village Nurse
Mar 6	Lever Brothers held their 8th AGM in *Bridge Inn*, Port Sunlight – previously held in London
May 8	Visit to Port Sunlight of 120 Germans, including a German Artillery Regimental Band
May 16	Port Sunlight Life-Saving and Swimming Society formed – over 300 men and 100 ladies as members
Jun 4	Consecration of the William Hesketh Lever Masonic Lodge (*see photo*)
Jun 21	An Art Exhibition in Hulme Hall was part of the festivities leading up to the Coronation
Jun 27	*Pennant House* grounds, Lr. Bebington, officially opened by Mrs Lever who planted a sapling oak
Jul 5	Open-air swimming baths opened at Port Sunlight (*see photo opposite*)
Jul 16	Port Sunlight Fire Brigade attended a haystack fire at *Eastham House Farm*
Jul 29	The Indian Native Army paid a visit to Port Sunlight (*see photo*)
Aug 9	Coronation Day was celebrated in Port Sunlight with a general holiday
Aug 26	First General meeting of the Port Sunlight Gymnastic Club
Sep 30	The Christ Church foundation stone was laid by Mrs Lever
Oct 8	First works surgery opened
Oct 8	Gymnasium opened by the Mayor of Birkenhead – built at a cost £3,067 [originally built on present War Memorial site] (*see photo*)
Dec 19	Annual Christmas treat in Hulme Hall for over 800 village children with Mr & Mrs Lever in attendance
—	Building converted into stables which later became the Fire Engine Station (in 1906)
—	Port Sunlight Cricket Club formed
—	Houses built: 11-17 & 64-70 Greendale Road; 9-17 Pool Bank and 2-18 Windy Bank (2-4 later moved)

The Indian Native Army seen parading through Port Sunlight Village on a visit 29 July 1902[PRG]

Above: *The cottage on the left is No.4 Windy Bank with No.2 next door designed by Grayson & Ould and built in 1902. When the Lady Lever Art Gallery was built, it was decided to open up the vista around the building so Nos.2-4 were later moved and the buildings in the background demolished*

Below: *The archway on the right in Windy Bank can also be seen in the centre of the picture above. From the left No.12 to No.2 Windy Bank on the right in their original position*

Above: *Freemasonry came to Port Sunlight with the consecration of the William Hesketh Lever Lodge No.2916 in the Grand Hall of the Schools in the presence of a large number of Brethren including many distinguished Masons holding Grand and Provisional rank from Cheshire, Lancashire, Staffordshire, Essex and elsewhere. After the installation of the Worshipful Master, the Brethren adjourned to the Bridge Inn for luncheon followed by loyal and Masonic toasts[PRG]*

Above: *The Gymnasium, which was opened on 8 October 1903 by the Mayor of Birkenhead. Built at a cost of £3,067 it originally stood on the site of the present War Memorial. It was moved in 1910 to the other side of the baths and later served as Mac Fisheries' Store before its demolition in the 1980s*

Right: *The Port Sunlight section Ist Royal Cheshire Engineers (Volunteers) whose headquarters were in Gladstone Hall are seen parading in the village*

Above: *Nos. 66-68 Greendale Road were built in 1902 and designed by Wilson & Talbot*

Above: *Nos. 11-17 Greendale Road, designed by the architect J Joseph Talbot and based on Kenyon Peel Hall in Lancashire [which has since been demolished], were built in 1902*

Right & Below: *The Open-air Swimming Bath at Port Sunlight was opened on 5 July 1902 by the Rt. Hon. Lord Stanmore GCMG in the presence of a large audience including Mr & Mrs Lever. The bath, which was situated at Ellen's Rocks near Greendale Road, was 100ft. in length, oval in shape and 75ft. at the widest point with a capacity of 225,000 gallons. The bath was glazed with green tiles, being 7ft. 3in. at the deep end and 3ft. 3in. at the other. The water came from the Port Sunlight Works, filtered and heated to 60 degrees. The thatched dressing rooms can be seen bottom right and the Gymnasium in its original position, can be seen beyond the Swimming Bath in the view below.*
The Port Sunlight Life-Saving and Swimming Society was formed on 16 May with over 300 men and 100 ladies as members. The cost of a swim to the residents was one penny

Jan 5   Church Drive Schools opened *(see photo opposite)*

Jan 12   Technical Institute opened (Hesketh Hall) *(see photo opposite)*

Jan 13   Initial gathering of the Mens' Meeting Mutual Improvement Society in Gladstone Hall

Jan 14   Mr & Mrs Lever held a Fancy Dress Ball for Port Sunlight children in Hulme Hall

Jan 19   Two new soaps launched: *Opera*, a small conveniently-sized tablet priced at one penny and *Plantol*, a high-class Toilet Soap recommended by doctors and skin specialists *(see photo)*

Feb 5   Six-day Licence to sell wine, spirits and beer granted to the Liverpool Public House Trust Co who had become the new tenants of the *Bridge Inn*

Apr 2   A public meeting of the Birkenhead & Wirral Women's Suffrage Society was held in Hulme Hall, presided over by Mr Lever [see 1913 when Mr Lever's house at Rivington was burnt down as a *protest by a Suffragette*]

Apr 3   First display given by the members of the Port Sunlight Gymnastic Club in Hulme Hall

Jun   *Coral Soap* introduced in 6 varieties

Jun 13   Auditorium opened as an open-air theatre by the Mayor of Bolton with an audience of almost 3,000 in attendance *(see photo opposite)*

Jul 18   The 1st Port Sunlight Company, The Boys' Brigade camp was held at Ramsey, Isle of Man

Jul 25   Port Sunlight Employees' Walking Competition was held *(see photo)*

Aug   Refined *Toilet Monkey Brand Soap* launched as a highly refined form of the well-known *Monkey Brand Soap* – composed of only the purest materials and entirely free from chemicals

Aug 1   Port Sunlight section of the Engineer Volunteers attended their Battalion camp at Beaumaris

Aug 20   The Men's Social Club decided to form a ping-pong team and suggested forming a Quoiting Club *(see photo)*

Aug 27   Lever Free Library and Museum opened (formerly the Girls' Hostel - later the Heritage Centre) – a gift from Mr Lever

Sep 1   Port Sunlight Ambulance Brigade formed

Sep 5   Port Sunlight Association Football Club celebrated the opening of their new ground in Pool Bank with a match against Everton FC which Everton won 5-0 *(see photo)*

—   Mr Lever sat on the Cheshire County Council

—   *Sunlight Soap* and *Lifebuoy Soap* now offered in octagonal tablets, retailing at 1d and 1/2d

—   Incognito visit by King Albert of the Belgians to Port Sunlight before his accession

—   The Port Sunlight Philharmonic Society was presented with a banner by the German chocolate firm of Stollwerk who visited the factory in 1903 *(see photo)*

Right: *The spectators are watching a match at the Port Sunlight Association Football Club's Pool Bank ground. The opening of this new ground on Saturday 5 September 1903 was celebrated when Mr Lever kicked off a friendly match against Everton FC (Everton won 5-0)* PRG

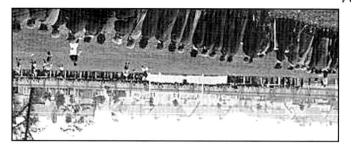

Above: The Port Sunlight Philharmonic Society are seen here in The Dell in 1903 with a banner which was presented by the German chocolate firm of Stollwerk from Cologne whose employees visited the factory in 1903. The leader, Mr John Cheshire is seated on the left next to the pianist Mr Fred Cheshire

Above: The male competitors are seen here in front of the General Offices 'ready for the off' at the start of the Port Sunlight Employees' Walking Competition which was held on 25 July 1903. The 27 mile course across the Wirral peninsula was completed in 4 hours 32 minutes by the mens' winner, and the ladies' winner took 2 hours 10 minutes to complete a shorter and less strenuous route PRG

Above: The two men on the right are playing quoits in front of the Men's Social Club whose members decided to form a Quoiting Club at a meeting on 20 August 1903. Quoiting here only lasted for seven years before the annex to the Social Club was built on the site of the Quoiting Ground in 1910. At the same meeting in 1903 a ping-pong team was started

Above: On 19 January 1903 Plantol Floral Bouquet[UNI] was launched by Lever Brothers, a high-class Toilet Soap recommended by doctors and skin specialists – contained no animal fat

Below: The dam (now Wharf Street) which separated the tidal creeks from Bromborough Pool. In the distance on the left is the Auditorium soon after construction, and on the right is the area later occupied by the rifle range and allotments (see page 33)PRG

Above: An exterior view of the Technical Institute (Hesketh Hall) which opened 12 January 1903 and was the gift of Mr Lever

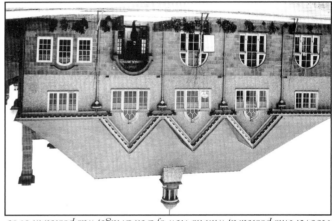

Above: The Auditorium, an open-air theatre, was built at one end of Dell Park. The entire floor to be occupied by the audience was cemented in and by using the natural slope of the bank there was seating accomodation for 2,400. However, when the Mayor of Bolton opened the venue on 13 June 1903 there was an estimated audience of almost 3,000.

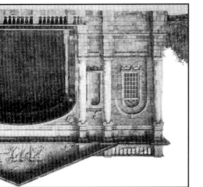

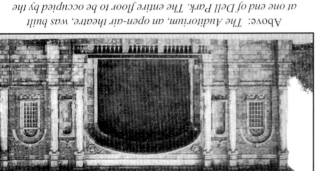

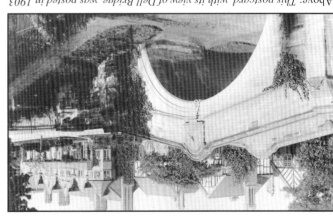

Above: This postcard, with its view of Dell Bridge, was posted in 1903

Below: Children playing at the rear of the Church Drive Schools. The original playground was built within the former tidal creek which was later filled in, leaving the playground considerably lower than the surrounding land PRG

Left: These children are posing in front of the Church Drive Schools, in Church Drive adjoining Christ Church. They were opened 5 January 1903 and provided additional school places to the Park Road Schools which had opened in 1896.

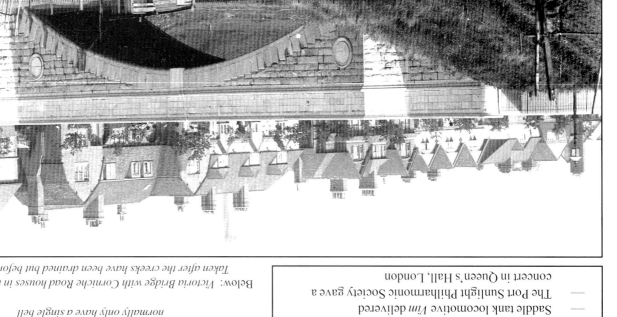

Below: Victoria Bridge with Corniche Road houses in the background. Taken after the creeks have been drained but before filling-in

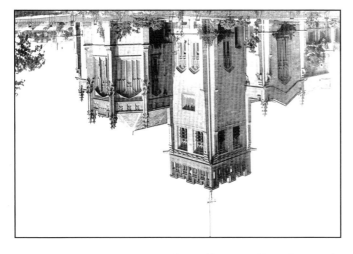

Above: Christ Church was opened by Mrs Lever on 8 June 1904 and normally would accommodate a congregation of 800 which could be increased to 1,000 when necessary. The Church was entered by two deeply-recessed doorways at the north-west. The nave, 104ft long by 30ft wide rose to a height of 32ft to 44ft, with open-timbered roofs. Inside the tower was a bell-ringer's floor and a belfry which contained a peal of eight bells. This was unusual for a free-church which would normally only have a single bell

Above: The foundation stone for Christ Church Port Sunlight was laid by Mrs Lever on 30 September 1902 It is seen here in the process of being built using Helsby red sandstone inside and out PRC

May 1	'Band Sunday' was recognised when the Village Prize Band accompanied by the Boy's Brigade paraded in full uniform and attended Church
May 23	Port Sunlight Football Club Committee arranged an Athletic Festival at the Pool Bank Football Ground
Jun 5	Last Sunday Service held in the Park Road Schools
Jun 8	Christ Church opened by Mrs Lever (*see photo*)
Jun 9	First wedding held in Christ Church
Jun 26	First time the Port Sunlight Sunday Schools' Anniversary was held in Christ Church
Jul 18	First sale of *Vim* scouring powder at 3d per canister
Jul 23	Over 50 boys of the Port Sunlight Boys' Brigade attended their annual camp at Ramsey, Isle of Man
Aug 23	New Levers' Motor Delivery Wagon service to trade customers started. Covering all Wirral and as far as Chester and Wrexham from Port Sunlight
Oct 14	Permission given by the Local Government Board for 6,647 sq yds surrounding the Church to be set aside as a burial ground - available for any employee (or member of his family) who had at least 15 years service
Dec	Reredos erected in Christ Church
—	*Sunlight Soap* offered a Gramophone and 3 records in exchange for 750 *Sunlight Soap* wrappers or 4,000 wrappers for a Half-Hunter Rolled Gold Watch (lady's or gentleman's)
—	A plaque was placed over the entrance of Gladstone Hall to commemorate its opening by Rt Hon WE Gladstone on 24 Nov 1891
—	*Capitol Toilet Soap* launched at 2d tablet in 4 perfumes:- Pink Rose, Honey, Old Brown Windsor and Glycerine & Cucumber
—	*Villa Toilet Soap* launched in three delicate perfumes - Pink Rose, Brown Windsor and Glycerine & Cucumber retailing at 1d per tablet
—	*Sealskin Toilet Soap*, especially suitable for tender skin and delicate complexions launched in Pink Rose, Lilac and Lemon at 2d per tablet
—	Two children's playgrounds were opened adjoining Church Drive
—	Saddle tank locomotive *Vim* delivered
—	The Port Sunlight Philharmonic Society gave a concert in Queen's Hall, London

Right: *The Port Sunlight Fire Brigade are seen outside the General offices with their steam-driven fire engine. The Brigade was in the charge of an experienced captain and composed of Lever Brothers' workers who were drilled periodically. Every provision was made against fire risks with an elaborate telephone system communicating all departments with the Central Switch Room. Small manual engines and fire buckets were available in each department and a further protection was provided throughout the works by fireproof doors and an automatic sprinkling system. A horse-drawn Ambulance Carriage was also kept at the fire station ready for use when required*

Above: *Seen here some time after their erection in 1899, three houses on the New Chester Road (158 on the right to 168 on the left) were the only ones in the village designed by the architect H Beswick*

Left: *A poster for Vim*(UNI) *scouring powder whose first sale at 3d per canister was on 18 July 1904. Before the introduction of Vim,*(UNI) *Monkey Brand Scouring Soap*(UNI) *had offered the best option for these regular household cleaning jobs*

Above: *In 1904 this iron frame was erected in front of The Auditorium and covered in canvas to protect the audience from the elements. In 1906 it was replaced with a slate roof.* PRG

Above: The 1905 Horticultural Society Show was held in the Auditorium seen here after the canvas cover was added PRG

Jan 1	Employees' Holiday Club and one-week's holiday with pay introduced
May	A slab of rock containing a footprint of the prehistoric *Cheirotherium Labyrinthodon*, found at Storeton Quarries, was presented to the Lever Museum
May	Allotments for juniors were provided in the village (*see photo opposite*)
Jul 5	Port Sunlight Rifle Club held its first shoot at the range between Victoria Bridge and the Pool Dam
Jul 7	Some 2,700 employees enjoyed an excursion to the Brussels International Exhibition and visited Lever's new Belgian factory at Forest
Jul 8	Trip to Blackpool for those not on the Belgian visit
Aug 24	First issue of Long Service Awards
Sep 8	Field Marshal Sir George White, VC, GCMG visited Port Sunlight - distinguished for the defence of Ladysmith in the Boer War
Oct 3-5	Port Sunlight Village Bazaar and Japanese Fete held in Church Drive Schools
Dec 21	First 1905 Staff Dance at *Thornton Manor*
Dec 28	Second 1905 Staff Dance at *Thornton Manor*
—	Estimated population of Port Sunlight 2,700
—	Launch of *Carnaval Toilet Soap* which had 3 perfumes (lilac, rose & violet) guaranteed pure and suitable for the most tender skin, retailing at 3d per tablet (*see advert*)
—	Launch of *Divan Turkish Bath Soap*, a new dainty perfumed toilet soap retailing at 2d per tablet
—	Construction started of No.3 Soapery
—	Management of *Bridge Inn* returned to residents'/ Lever Bros Committee
—	Saddle tank locomotive *Lifebuoy* delivered to Port Sunlight
—	Port Sunlight Ambulance Division was founded - organised and equipped at the expense of Lever Brothers
—	Employees' Benefit Fund Established – pensions for male employees retiring at 65 and women at 60.
—	Lever Brothers introduced Long Service Awards
—	The 'Employees' Holiday Club' was encouraged by the company
—	Buildings completed: 10-16 & 1-47 Boundary Road; 6-13 Church Drive and 1-9 Underley Terrace

Above: This advert for Carnaval Soap, which was launched in 1905 and retailed at 3d per tablet, appeared in a Lever Brothers' "Souvenir" publication.

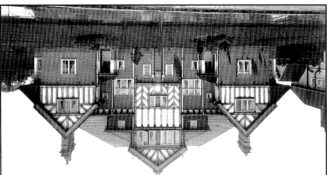

Carnaval.—Lever Brothers' latest creation in Toilet Soaps is a dainty soap, made of the best materials that it is possible to buy for use in soap-making, carefully selected and tested for their purity and quality. It is exquisitely scented in three of the perfumes most appreciated, and is altogether a soap suited to the most fastidious of users. It forms a necessary and charming addition to every lady's toilet, as it is suitable for the most tender skin and delicate complexion. It is attractively put up in art cartons containing three tablets, elegantly wrapped, and is made in three choice perfumes, à la Violette, a la Rose, au Lilas.

In 1905 Levers constructed some larger houses on 'The Wiend' which were apparently specifically for managers and supervisors – both pictures above are of the houses in The Wiend taken not long after their completion

Above: No.3 Soapery in the process of being constructed, photographed on 25 March 1905 with New Chester Road in the background (completed October 1906)

Above: Many of the houses in Boundary Road, Port Sunlight were completed in 1905 including Nos. 19-25. The sundial was one of several around the village which have since disappeared

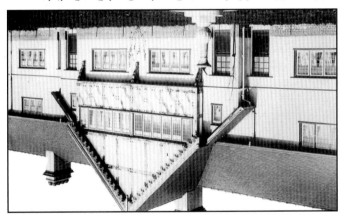

Right: On 8 September Field Marshal Sir George White, Hero of the Boer War visited Port Sunlight. This sundial which still stands on Bath Street is said to have been originally erected by local residents to commemorate the Relief of Mafeking in the Boer War

Right: The name "Irish Express" was given to the little narrow gauge railway engines that hauled the earth wagons from factory workings to fill in the creeks and waterways in Port Sunlight Village. There were 5 engines used continuously from 1905 to 1914 until the last journey just before the Royal Visit of that year.PRG

Above: In May 1905 allotment gardens were provided exclusively for juniors.' It was soon a common thing after school hours " to see a crowd of busy, energetic young gardeners hard at work with spade and rake, digging and planting.PRG

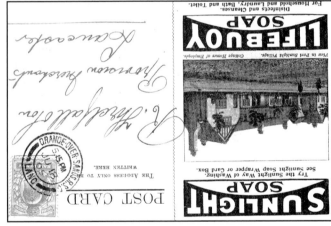

Above: Lever Brothers used many ways of marketing their products. This postcard advertised Sunlight Soap & Lifebuoy Soap on one half with space for an address on the other half. The reverse side was blank except for the company's name – which on this one was :- 'Entwistle's Mikado Tea House, Italian Warehousemen, Kents Bank Road, Grange-Over-Sands'

Left: Port Sunlight Ambulance Brigade seen here after their triumph on 17 July at the Ormskirk Carnival where they won all five of the teapots offered as prizes! Seen here: Messrs. Atkinson (Captain), Mills, Lewis, Ratcliffe and Morrison PRG

Jan 24 — Mr Lever was elected Liberal MP for Wirral Division of Cheshire by a majority of 1,701 votes

Jan 29 — Employees' Holiday Club AGM reported that 2,147 employees had taken a week's holiday with pay

Feb 2 — A Chinese conjuror 'performed some marvellous feats' at the Auditorium

Feb 20 — Mr Lever MP made his maiden speech in the House of Commons

Mar 1 — Baths & Rest Room for females started in factory

Mar 31 — One of the finest Gymnastic Displays ever held in Wirral was given in the Auditorium and attended by Mr & Mrs Lever

Apr 12 — Nearly 150 officers and crew of the Japanese battleship *Katori* were guests at Port Sunlight (see photo opposite)

Apr 23 — Port Sunlight AFC won the Wirral Senior Cup

May 10 — Mr Lever MP introduced a Private Member's Bill to provide old age pensions (passed 1st & 2nd reading but lapsed due to lack of time. Following year old age pensions introduced for persons over 70 years of age whose income was less than £31.10.0 per year [60p per week]

Jul — The Port Sunlight Ambulance Division was registered

Jul — Lever Brothers purchased Hodgson & Simpson the old established firm of soap makers who were based in Wakefield

Jul 12 — The Bandstand was opened on 'The Diamond', when the Port Sunlight Prize Band performed an interesting musical selection (see photo)

Jul 21 — Athletic Sports of the Port Sunlight employees were held at Wirral Park, Bebington [now the Oval]

Aug — The original stables [behind the present Heritage Centre] were converted into a Fire Engine Station which was manned by 2 officers and 12 firemen

Aug 9 — Some 2,000 Levers' employees travelled by the *Prince of Wales* and *Mona's Isle* to Douglas in the Isle of Man for their annual excursion

Sep — *Comfort*, a new laundry soap made from pure sweet oils extracted from seeds, fruits and nuts was launched

Sep — The *Daily Mail* and other papers began their campaign against the so-called Soap Trust

Sep 1 — Port Sunlight Football Club began the new season in the Lancashire Combination on the new Wirral Park ground

Sep 6 — Delegates and friends of the Trades Union Congress numbering some 600 visit Port Sunlight

Oct — No.3 Soapery completed

Oct — Port Sunlight Internal Railway and Wharf completed

Oct — Employees' Works Divisional Committees formed

Oct 1 — The Vinolia Co Ltd was taken over by Levers and in 1907 production was transferred to Port Sunlight

Dec 4 — Writ issued by Lever Brothers Limited against Associated Newspapers Ltd, proprietors of the *Daily Mail* and Pictorial Newspapers Co Ltd, proprietors of the *Daily Mirror*

— Auditorium given a permanent slate roof (see photo opposite) replacing the temporary canvas covering

Houses built: 3-4 Brook Street; 2-14, 36-72 Central Road; 18-26 Circular Drive; 15-27 & 35-59 Lower Road; 2-6 Pool Bank and 11-35 Primrose Hill

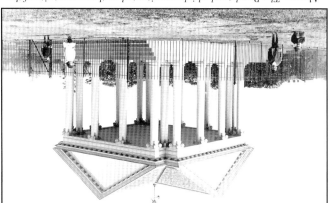

Above: The Port Sunlight Ambulance Division was registered in August and their horse-drawn ambulance was housed in the old stables which were converted in 1906 into the Fire Engine Station manned by 2 officers and 12 firemen

Above: This election vehicle on behalf of the founder of the Company, Mr William Hesketh Lever, who stood as the Liberal candidate for the Wirral Division in January 1906, is loaded with voters who helped Mr Lever triumph at his fourth attempt to become a Member of Parliament. Mr Lever was elected Liberal MP for Wirral Division of Cheshire by a majority of 1,701 votes

PRG

Above: The Bandstand which was situated on the present site of the Art Gallery was opened on 12 July 1906, when the Port Sunlight Prize Band performed an interesting musical selection. The high metal fence surrounding it kept the children away. It was later moved (see page 36) to its present position on 'The Diamond' when the centre of the village was redesigned in 1910

Above: *Originally there were two groups of shops in Boundary Road. These two were numbered 1 & 3 and stood at the end nearest Bebington Road. Together with the houses behind, they were damaged by bombing during the last war. Rebuilt, they are now houses. The four boys in front of the shop are all wearing plus-fours in this 1906 photograph. The shop on the left apparently specialised in the repair of umbrellas and later became the village surgery and home to Port Sunlight Sick Club*

Above: *Nearly 150 officers and crew of the Japanese Battleship* Katori, *which had docked at Birkenhead, were guests at Port Sunlight on 12 April 1906 and are seen here marching through Port Sunlight Village, flanked by enthusiastic villagers and their children*[PRG]

Above: *These shops at the New Chester Road end of Boundary Road, Nos. 33 & 35, are still there today*

Above: *The children are playing on a bank in front of Nos.1-11 Brook Street designed by Grayson & Ould and built in 1901 and 1906*

Above: *The Auditorium's temporary iron frame and canvas roof was replaced in 1906 with a slate roof as seen here*

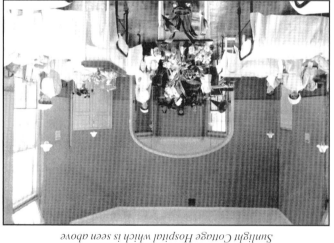

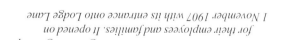

Above: Lever Brothers built The Port Sunlight Cottage Hospital for their employees and families. It opened on 1 November 1907 with its entrance onto Lodge Lane

Below: A scene on one of the wards in the new Port Sunlight Cottage Hospital which is seen above

Above: This 1907 picture is of girls and boys from the Church Drive School who are exercising with dumbbells in the Main Hall

Above Right: Church Drive School Infants posing in their classroom for the photographer

Right: Park Road School Infants having a tea party with their friends in this photograph taken in 1907

Mar 18 Lever Brothers commenced proceedings for infringement of their trade mark 'Sunlight' against Mr AE Scott proprietor of shops in Manchester who was also Chairman of The Titan Soap Co Ltd - shortly before the hearing, the defendant approached Levers with a view to a settlement and ultimately the defendant agreed to an injunction which the Court granted with costs

May 16 The Mersey Railway Company started a bus service between Port Sunlight and Rock Ferry Station which proved popular at 1d for the 2 mile journey (see poster opposite)

Jul 8 The House of Lords made a judgement against the Mersey Railway Co, and the bus service between Port Sunlight & Rock Ferry Station was stopped

Jul 17 Three-day trial began following the writ issued in December 1906 against the *Daily Mail* and *Daily Mirror* –

Although Mr William Lever had been advised by 2 eminent counsel that an action for Libel would not succeed, he refused to accept their judgement and summoned FE Smith [an old boy of Birkenhead School, later to become Lord Birkenhead] whose opinion was "There is no answer to this action for libel, and the damages must be enormous" – settlement arrived at on 19 July and agreed damages of £50,000 (increased by other actions to £91,000) awarded to Levers against the *Daily Mail* & *Daily Mirror*

Oct Rev S Gamble-Walker, Port Sunlight's first Minister, announced he had accepted the call to a Church in Blackpool

Nov 1 The Cottage Hospital in Lodge Lane opened in Port Sunlight for employees and families (see photo)

Nov 15 Gale & Pouldon gave a cinematograph display in the Auditorium of the Army and Navy, plus two humorous films

— Estimated population of Port Sunlight 3,600

— Houses built: 1-27 Central Road; 29-33 Lower Road; 8-34 Pool Bank; 1-9 Primrose Hill and 23-24 Windy Bank

Above: Members of the Port Sunlight Gymnastic Club, which was founded in 1902, were pictured in a 1907 "Souvenir of Port Sunlight" booklet and described as 'The Champion Eight Instructor'. They are pictured by parallel bars with boxing gloves, basket ball, fencing foils and masks, and Indian clubs. The gymnasium was opened in 1902 and by 1907 the membership had reached about 200. The 1907 display by 150 athletes from leading clubs in the Liverpool and Birkenhead areas in the Auditorium, was described as being the largest and most successful ever held in the district – events included:- Cavalry Sword Exercises, Horizontal and Parallel Bars, Wrestling, High Jumping, Rope Climbing Competition and ended with an exhibition game of Basket Ball

Right: The poster is advertising a railway omnibus service which was started in May 1907 by the Mersey Railway Company as a "feeder" for the railways. The fare from Port Sunlight to Rock Ferry Station was one penny for the two-mile journey and there was an intermediate stage from The Dell to the Station for a halfpenny. The buses ran every 12 minutes and travelled along New Chester Road, into Port Sunlight Village at Bolton Road with a stop at the Bridge Inn. The new service proved popular, especially with employees travelling from Liverpool. The alternative transport then was a tram which went as far as the New Ferry Toll Bar. But the bus venture was destined to have a very short life. A judgement in the House of Lords given on the 8 July 1907 went against the Mersey Railway, and the service stopped on that day. Despite the success of an appeal which required an undertaking that bus passengers would be carried only to or from a railway station, the service was not reintroduced.

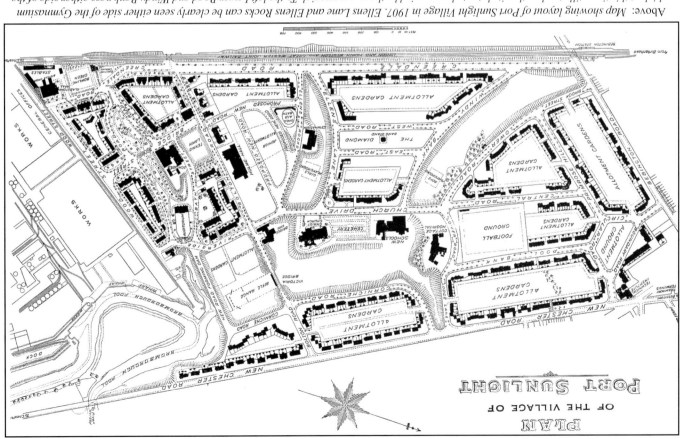

Above: Map showing layout of Port Sunlight Village in 1907. Ellens Lane and Ellens Rocks can be clearly seen either side of the Gymnasium which at this time still stood on the site later to be occupied by the war memorial. To the left Lower Road and Windy Bank pass either side of the site where the Art Gallery was started six years later

Jan — RS Hudson Ltd of West Bromwich and Liverpool was purchased by Lever Brothers. Well known for its brand names of *Omo* (introduced in 1908) and later *Rinso* (1910) to be marketed under Hudson's name but made at Port Sunlight

Feb 26 — Visit of 400 Wholesale Buying Agents with lunch served in the Auditorium

Apr — First sale of Lever's *Easy Shaving Stick*

Aug 29 — Some 3,000 Lever Brothers Employees enjoyed an outing from Port Sunlight to the Franco-British Exhibition in London

Aug 30 — Mr JD Lever's elder son, James Darcy, celebrated his 21st Birthday (both father and son were called James Darcy)

Sep — Lever Brothers appointed soapmakers to His Majesty King Edward VII

Sep 5 — Employees' excursion to Belle Vue Manchester

Oct 31 — Over the previous 12 months 59,860 visitors had been shown through the works

— Port Sunlight Rugby Club was founded (known in the early days as the 'Cosmopolitans') - they are still in existence but are now based at Leverhulme Sports Field, Green Lane

— Readers of the Lever Bros magazine *Progress* were offered the chance of winning £1.10 shillings first prize and 15 shillings second prize for a photograph of the best dressed window containing only Lever Bros products. Grocers with the best window displays received gifts including a piano, grocers' fittings, bicycles, typewriters, check tills etc

— Lever Brothers also appointed soapmakers to the Prince of Wales, and the Kings of Siam, Turkey, Portugal and Spain

— Bromborough Port Estate Ltd company formed

— Higher Education scheme introduced for young employees

Above: Members of the Port Sunlight Ambulance Brigade pictured on a visit to Thornton Manor

LEVER BROTHERS LIMITED,
BY APPOINTMENT
SOAPMAKERS TO HIS MAJESTY THE KING.

Left: Lever Brothers were appointed soapmakers to His Majesty King Edward VII and continued to display the Royal Coat of Arms on their products and advertising material /PRG

Below: The Co-Partners' Club, colloquially known as 'The Pavilion' is pictured in the centre of the picture with the bowling green to the left and the quoiting area in the foreground. Although a set of railway signals can be seen on the right, Port Sunlight Station has not yet been built. No.3 Soapery can just be seen in the distance over the top of the main offices on the left

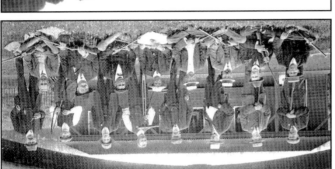

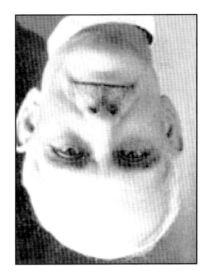

Above: *Rev Lewis Henry Mills appointed minister of Christ Church Port Sunlight*

Right: *Photographed by George Davies, Port Sunlight's photographer, from close to his home on New Chester Road, this major fire in the resin fields was brought under control in under three hours*

Right: *Members of the Port Sunlight Rifle Club pictured in front of Victoria Bridge c.1909. One of the creeks ran under this bridge until it was cut off. After it was drained the rifle range was built under the bridge* PRG

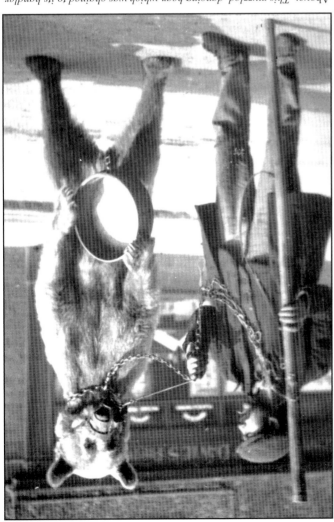

Above: *This muzzled, dancing bear, which was chained to its handler was photographed by George Davies outside his shop in New Chester Road in 1909 and sold as postcards with the caption "Teddy Bear at Port Sunlight". It must have been a frightening sight. This was the opinion of Ena Stanley writing in her "Memories of Old Eastham" about that time – "A man dressed as a Russian came with a performing bear. I think we were all scared and he did not come again"*

1909

Feb 25 Details of the Co-Partnership scheme made public by Mr Lever at a special meeting in The Auditorium

Mar 25 Mr W Hulme Lever celebrated his 21st birthday

Apr 21 Fire broke out in the Resin Fields and was under control in under 3 hours *(see photo)*

May 1 Lever Brothers Co-Partnership Trust formed

May 16 New Minister, Rev Lewis H Mills, appointed Minister of Christ Church

Jun 20 Sunday School Anniversary Service when over 1,200 children gathered in the Auditorium

Jul The Village Band, in their new uniforms, gave a concert at the Auditorium for the 'Birkenhead Dock Disaster Fund'

Jul The members of the Port Sunlight Swimming Society and the Port Sunlight Gymnastic Club are given permission to use the lake, created from ponds on Mr Lever's *Thornton Manor Estate*, at certain times

Jul 7 The "Cosmopolitans" accepted the Company's offer to share the Pool Bank ground with the Football Club

Jul 8 Three William Hulme Lever Scholarships of £10 each set up for boys and girls in the Port Sunlight Schools

Jul 10 Between 4,000 and 6,000 Levers' Port Sunlight employees enjoyed a day out to Blackpool

Jul 23 First distribution of Co-Partnership Certificates

Aug 30 The Auditorium was opened for the day as a Roller Skating Rink with a professional instructor

Dec 3 Mr Lever ceased to be a Member of Parliament when Parliament was dissolved

— Memorial East Window installed in Christ Church in memory of James & Eliza Lever

— A new book *Labour and Housing at Port Sunlight* was published by Mr WL George

— The West Wing of the General Office was extended to include new offices for directors and managers, a girls' rest room and new laboratory

1910

Mar — No.4 Soapery and a new printing plant started

Mar 7 — The Social and Bowling Club, with its new extension on the site of the old Quoiting Ground, was reopened by Mr and Mrs Lever (see photo)

Mar 29 — Mr James Darcy Lever senior, the other brother in Lever Brothers Ltd died at *Thornton House*, Thornton Hough

May 6 — **King Edward VII died**

Jun 17/19 — Port Sunlight employees' Excursion to Brussels

Aug 2 — Girls' Dining Room opened in No.3 Soapery

Oct — The Bandstand was moved to the centre of 'The Diamond' *(see photo)*

Nov — The second locomotive to bear the name *Sydney* was delivered new to Port Sunlight. (It bore the name until 1914 when, renamed *King George*, it pulled the Royal train for the visit of King George & Queen Mary

Dec — A New Men's Dining Hall inside the works was opened in the former printing room - this meant that Gladstone Hall was vacated and was then put to many uses including the Girls' Social Club

— A Competition for a revised layout plan for the village resulted in 'The Diamond' which still forms the central feature of Port Sunlight Village

— Completion of filling in creeks throughout the village resulted in Victoria Bridge near the *Bridge Inn* being buried. The parapets were reused on the New Chester Road Bridge over the extended railway

— The Gymnasium was moved to its new position alongside the swimming baths

— East Wing of the General Offices extended

— Levers' Private Railway was extended to Bromborough Port, over Spital Dam *(see photo)*, underneath the New Chester Road, and through 'Rainbow Cutting' alongside Magazine Road

— Lever Brothers acquired Edward Cook & Co Ltd soap makers based in Lynn and Norwich, and John Barrington Ltd, soap makers based in Dublin

— Saddle tank locomotive *Lux* delivered for use at Port Sunlight (later renamed *Princess Mary*)

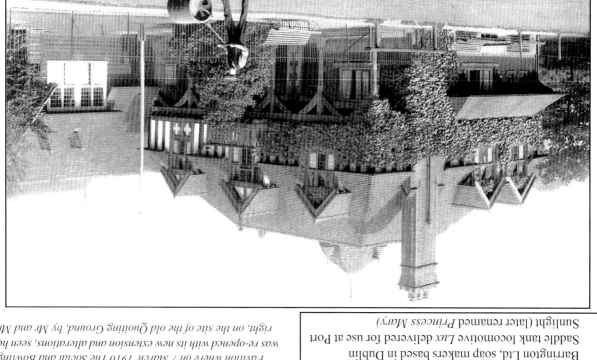

Below: The groundsman is rolling the Bowling Green in front of the Pavilion where on 7 March 1910 The Social and Bowling Club was re-opened with its new extension and alterations, seen here on the right, on the site of the old Quoiting Ground, by Mr and Mrs Lever.

Above: This picture shows the girls of the Lux Packing Department with their hair tucked under their bonnets and their overalls elaborately gathered from the yoke

Above: The roof of the Bandstand, supported on a wooden frame, is about to be moved on a wooden track from its original position on the site of the Lady Lever Art Gallery (see 1906) to the centre of The Diamond PRG

Above: One of the most important works with regard to the development of Bromboro Port Estate was the construction of a railway from the Chester to Birkenhead line. It connected the main line at Port Sunlight sidings through part of Lever Brothers' Estate and the Bromborough Port Estate to near the banks of the River Mersey. To achieve this, the ferro-concrete culvert pictured here took the waters of the Bromborough Mill Pool and the River Dibbin under an embankment some 40ft. higher than the dam, and strong enough to carry the railway line. Seen here, the construction of the culvert is well advanced (for a completed picture of the project see page 39).

Above: Plan of Port Sunlight Village from 1910 showing the redesigned centre of the village with its very formal intersecting straight avenues which later became Queen Mary's and King George's Drives and The Causeway

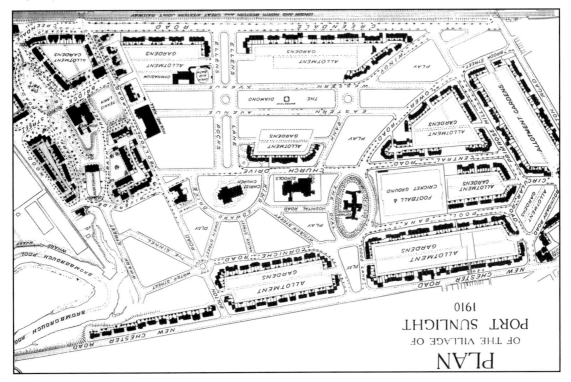

Above: *Lever Brothers' van pictured here had a steam engine driven with paraffin. It engaged in delivery work on Merseyside and the Wirral Peninsula, being the only one of its kind operated by the Company. The boiler was under the driver's seat and steam billowed out from beneath the chassis. The driver on the left was William Gray with his assistant John Woods on the right* PRG

Right: *A copy of the Late Thomas Brocklebank's Estate Sale Catalogue which included the Storeton Quarry Railway*

Above: *The Co-partner Bowlers are competing in a competition in front of their club*

Above: *The Port Sunlight Rugby Club was founded as the "Cosmopolitans" in 1908 and in 1909 shared the Pool Bank field with the Football team. This is a photograph taken on their 1911 tour to the Isle of Man —*

Left to right, standing, back row: R Smith, A Powell (captain), T Ogden, A J Davies, H Podmore, F Statham, WS Clough and AJ Gordon sitting, left bench: RCR Shand, J Dodd, N Higson, J Hughes and G Davey; right bench: W Smith, B Marsden, J Knight and RA Thomas; sitting on ground: CM Higson, J Lemon and AN Other PRG

Jan	Soap-making capacity increased to 4,000 tons weekly
Apr 6	Hulme Hall Art Gallery opened to display Mr Lever's Art Collection
Jun 22	King George V & Queen Mary's Coronation Day was celebrated in Port Sunlight Village with festivities extending over 3 days and all school children receiving a commemorative medal
Jul 6	WH Lever was created a Baronet - his name appearing in the list of Coronation Honours for King George V
Sep	Following the death of Thomas Brocklebank, the Storeton Estate, including the Storeton Tramway was put up for auction and acquired by Sir William Lever (see poster)
Nov 9	The new stage at Gladstone Hall used for theatrical purpose for the first time with a performance of Port Sunlight Children's Operata *Jan of Windmill Land*
Dec 20	Lever Brothers acquired Hazelhurst & Sons, old established soapmakers of Runcorn
Dec 21	The Philharmonic and Amateur Orchestral Societies of Port Sunlight performed *The Messiah* in the Auditorium
Dec 28	A Memorial Window in the North Transept at Christ Church was dedicated to the memory of James Darcy Lever by his brother Sir William Lever
—	A Separate Research Laboratory was established in the Port Sunlight works (*see photo opposite*)
—	No.4 Soapery completed
—	Cinematographic projection room and new entrance added to the north end of Gladstone Hall
—	Houses built: 16-34 Central Road

Above: A poster for the Cosmopolitan Rugby Club (which later changed its name to the Port Sunlight Rugby Club in 1920)^PRG

Above: Seen here before the addition of the projection room in 1911, Gladstone Hall was originally used as the Men's Dining Hall, but in 1910 a new Mens' Dining Hall inside the works had been opened in the former printing room - this meant that Gladstone Hall was vacated and could be put to many uses including the Girls' Social Club

Above: These two blocks of cottages in Central Road numbering from 16 on the right to 34 in the background on the left were the only houses in the road to be completed in 1911

Above: The railway engine is crossing the finished embankment which was built some 40 ft. higher than the Bromborough Mill Pool through which run the waters run on their way to the River Mersey^PRG

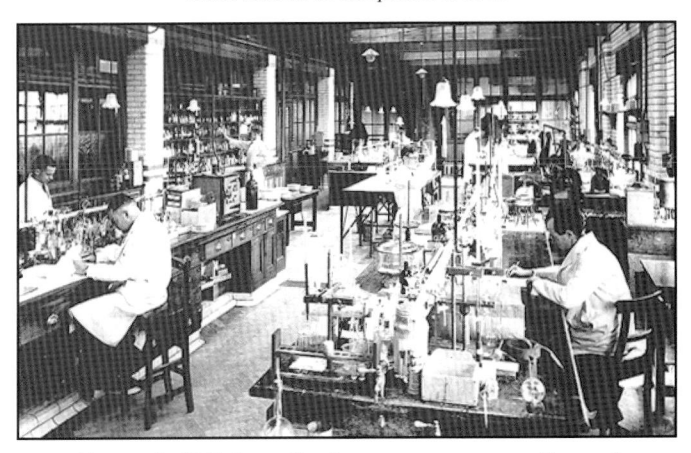

Above: In 1911 Lever Brothers set up a separate Research Laboratory in the Port Sunlight works in the 'flat iron' building

Above: This view was taken in 1902 when Hulme Hall was used to display part of William Lever's Art Collection as part of the Coronation festivities. In April 1911 the hall was once again used as a gallery prior to the building of the Lady Lever Art gallery^PRG

Right: Girls Social Club Drill Class

Jan 5   Mr FS Moore was appointed Captain of the No.2 (Port Sunlight) Company of the National Reserve

Mar 12 The marriage of Mr J Darcy Lever (son of Mr James D Lever senior) to Miss Annie Maud King took place at St George's Congregational Church, Thornton Hough - Port Sunlight village was bedecked in flags for the occasion

Mar 14 During the national coal strike, Lever Brothers had several weeks stock and were able to offer villagers coal from the Works at 1/- per cwt.

Apr   Candle manufacture commenced at Port Sunlight – candle factory erected

Apr 24 Mr W Hulme Lever, son of Sir William Hesketh Lever, married Miss Marion Bryce-Smith (*see photo*)

Jul   It was announced that Lever Brothers had been appointed Soapmakers to His Majesty the King of the Hellenes

Jul 20 Visit to Port Sunlight by Prime Minister Rt Hon HH Asquith (*see photo*)

Jul 27 The 1st Port Sunlight Company, The Boys' Brigade, set off for their annual camp at Sir William and Lady Lever's estate at Rivington near Bolton

Nov   First sale of *Swan Bleach*

Nov 12 Lever Brothers' Chairman, Sir William Lever and Lady Lever set off on a business tour of Africa

—   Houses built: 64-78 Bolton Road & 1-21 Water Street

Above: *The wedding of William Hulme Lever, only son of Sir William Hesketh Lever and Lady Lever, to Marion Bryce-Smith on 24 April 1912*

Above: *Sir William & Lady Lever lead the 1912 Sunday School Anniversary Parade through Port Sunlight Village*

Above: *The Prime Minister the Rt. Hon.Mr Asquith visits Port Sunlight on 20 July 1912*

Above: *The Boys' Brigade Band leads the Church Parade procession along Greendale Road*

Left: *This 1912 advertisement shows the variety of products produced by Lever Brothers at that time*[UNI]

Right: *In 1912 the decision was made to cut through the neck of the land where the River Dibbin entered Bromborough Pool. This gave easier access for vessels entering Port Sunlight Dock without having to pass barges moored at the wharf. This picture, taken from the New Chester Road, shows the mammoth task of cutting through the sandstone bedrock to form the new channel* (See map below)

Below: *This plan of Bromborough Pool and the Port Sunlight wharves shows the area (shaded black) which was cut away in 1912 to improve access for vessels entering and leaving Port Sunlight Dock* (see photo right). *Barges continued to sail around the resultant island, known as 'Wharf Island' until the remains of the pool were eventually filled in*

Below: *Seen here, the original Bromborough Pool Bridge which carried the New Chester Road over the tidal inlet*

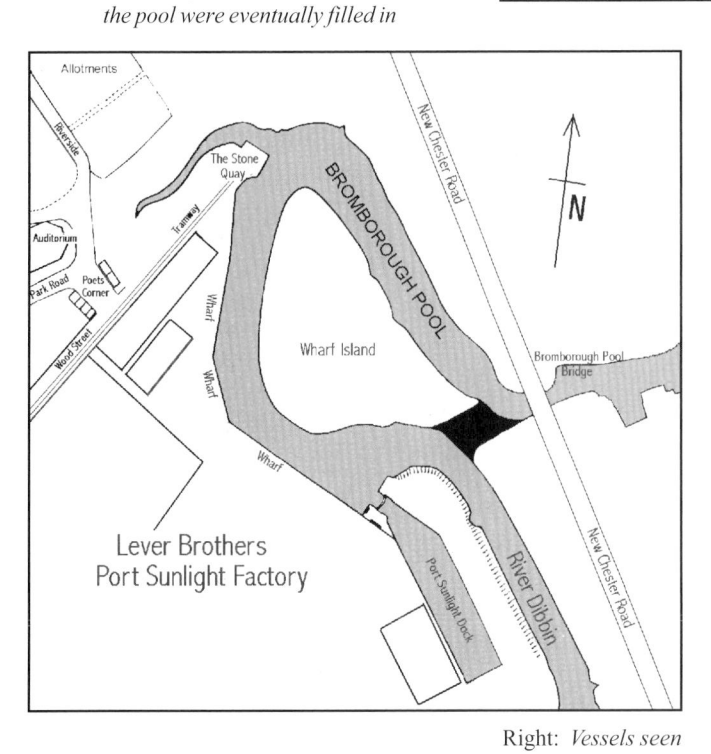

Right: *Vessels seen here passing under the original Bromborough Pool Bridge after the new channel has been created*[PRG]

Below: *Garden parties for employees and their families were a regular event at* Thornton Manor. *Seen here, Port Sunlight Children's Choir are pictured at the Co-Partners' Garden Party*

Below: *Estate Department Football team 1912*[PRG]

Above: Players and officials of the Port Sunlight Association Football Club are pictured in the 1912/13 season – some of the players then were:- H Pyatt, L Pyatt, G Jones, H Mercer, R Lloyd, W Jackson, J Bamford, C Gayner, J McWilliam, J Norbury, J Waters, C Ansell, J Maddocks & Mr Roberts, G Locker (trainer) and officials:- WH McWilliam, J Haines & Tom Wood PRG

Jan	18	Port Sunlight Prize Band won first prize at Dolgelly
Jan	28	Miss Alice Hesketh Lever (daughter of the late Mr James D Lever) married Mr John Fitzgerald Cream, JP
Feb	8	*Mrs Gorringe's Necklace* was the first appearance on stage of the Port Sunlight Players' Club
Mar	11	Sir William and Lady Lever arrive home from their Africa Tour
Apr	9	Elizabeth Ruth Lever, daughter of Mr & Mrs William Hulme Lever, was born
May		Port Sunlight Division of the St John's Ambulance Brigade erected Ambulance cupboards at various points in Port Sunlight Village, Bebington and Bromborough
Jun	13	It was announced that Sir William Hesketh Lever Bart. had been granted the Order of Leopold II by his Majesty King Albert of the Belgians in recognition of his services to the Belgian Congo
Jun	29	The annual Christ Church Anniversary Service and Procession took place in Port Sunlight Village (see photo)
Jul	1	Nigerian Chiefs visit Port Sunlight
Jul	8	*The Bungalow*, Lever's home at Rivington near Bolton, was burnt down by a suffragette - despite Lever's personal support for the cause (see photo - also 2 April 1903)
Jul	24	**Death of Lady Lever** was received with great sorrow throughout Port Sunlight Village and further afield including a telegram from the King and Queen. After her death, Sir William Lever said "I am convinced that without her great influence there would have been neither a Port Sunlight, nor a Lever Brothers as we know it today"
Sep	8	Girls' Social Club opened in 'The Diamond' - replaced the Girls' Institute over the Co-operative Shop which then became the Collegium
Sep	13	Sir William Lever sailed from Liverpool on his 4th round-the-world voyage
Dec	1	New Saddle tank locomotive *Alberta* delivered
—		Marble statue 'L'Opprime Prenant Conscience de Sa Force' by AG Guilleux unveiled outside the Art Gallery - it was originally in Sir William Lever's garden at *Thornton Manor*
—		Houses built: 1-22 King George's Drive; 23-50 Queen Mary's Drive, 8-17 The Causeway and 19-22 Windy Bank

Above: One of several semi-detached houses built by Levers in 1913 on the Old Chester Road opposite to where the Oval stands today

Above: The Girls' Social Club opened in 'The Diamond' on 8 September 1913. It replaced the Girls' Institute over the Co-operative Shop on the corner of Bridge Street and Bolton Road which then became 'The Collegium'

Above: This 'George Davies' postcard of Lodge Lane Port Sunlight was posted from No.15 on 8 September 1913

Above: On 8 July 1913 Sir William & Lady Lever's Bungalow at Rivington, near Bolton, was burned by the suffragette Edith Rigby, despite his personal support for the cause (see April 1903)

Above: *The Lever Brothers' Co-Partners posing with Sir William & Lady Lever in front of* Thornton Manor

Above: *Port Sunlight Boys' Brigade line the path to Christ Church on the occasion of Lady Lever's funeral*

Above: *The Bandstand on its new site on The Diamond is partly hidden behind the trees*

Above: *This was view taken in front of the General Offices after the removal of the Storeton Tramway rail track which ran parallel with the building. The Storeton Tramway was acquired from the late Thomas Brocklebank's Estate in 1911 and was immediately ripped out*

Right: *The Causeway, with Christ Church in the background, was photographed in Port Sunlight Village on 20 June 1913 by George Davies, the well-known Port Sunlight photographer*

Above: *The Villagers here are watching the Christ Church Sunday School Anniversary procession on the Diamond 29 June 1913. On the right is the site later to be occupied by the Village War Memorial*

Mar	Final journey by the little railway engine which was one of 5 known by the villagers as the 'Irish Express' which had completed the filling in of the ravines in the village with material excavated from the factory
Mar 23	No.1 Motor Fire Engine acquired
Mar 25	King George V and Queen Mary visited the factory and village and laid the foundation stone of the Art Gallery accompanied by the Earl & Countess of Derby. King George's and Queen Mary's Drives were named in honour of their visit (*see photos opposite*)
Mar 25	A Private Halt was officially opened at Port Sunlight on the Birkenhead to Chester railway line
May 5	Passenger train service for employees at Bromboro Port commenced
May 23	Memorial West Window, dedicated to Lady Lever, unveiled in Christ Church by her brother John Hulme
Jun 30	A & F Pears Ltd, makers of *Pears Soap* taken over by Lever Brothers Ltd
Jul 15	Fifty representatives of German cities received a welcoming reception together with 15 other nationalities at Port Sunlight – not knowing that just 3 weeks later the First World War would start
Aug 4	WAR DECLARED: Volunteer units raised for active service
Aug 7	Nineteen members of the Port Sunlight St John's Ambulance left for the south of England
Sep 6	'God Speed' service for the first 700 Port Sunlight men of the Wirral Battalion held at the Auditorium
Sep 7	Thousands say farewell to the Port Sunlight men of the Wirral Battalion who left for Chester
Sep 14	First Port Sunlight Village war casualty killed in action
Oct	It was announced that Lever Brothers had received the Royal Warrant as Soapmakers to HM the Queen Mother of Italy, Margherita de Savoie
Oct	Sir WH Lever's collection of art treasurers were removed from Hulme Hall to accommodate 111 Belgian refugees who were the guests of Port Sunlight for 5 weeks. Hulme Hall was later used as a Military Hospital
Nov 19	A Roll of Honour was exhibited at Port Sunlight which contained the 1,670 names of the men who 'answered their country's call' (*see photo*)
Dec 4	The Narthex, a canopied structure with vaulted roof, containing the tomb of Lady Lever was unveiled by her husband. It was added to the West End of Christ Church under the Memorial West Window dedicated to Lady Lever (and now contains bronze effigies of Lady Lever & Lord Leverhulme)
—	Lever Central Office – South Wing Offices completed
—	Parts of the Port Sunlight factory turned over to war production
—	Port Sunlight AFC were champions of the First Division Wirral Combination
—	Houses built: 60-62 Bolton Road; 1-35 The Ginnel and 2-4 Water Street

Above: *This was the elaborate cover for the Official Souvenir Brochure to celebrate the visit of King George V and Queen Mary to Port Sunlight on 25 March 1914. It included an artist's impression of the Lady Lever Art Gallery for which the Royal visitors laid the Foundation Stone* (see photo on page 46)

Right: *A Roll of Honour was exhibited at Port Sunlight on 19 November 1914 which contained the 1,670 names of the men who 'answered their country's call'*

Below: *The postcard caption read "Port Sunlight. Waiting for the King". The Boys' Brigade look very smart lined up behind Hulme Hall to meet the King and Queen*

Above: *The Royal party are about to pass underneath the welcoming banners draped between temporary columns outside Hesketh Hall as the crowd watch them pass with eager anticipation*

Above: *The royal car passes in front of Lever Brothers' general offices flanked by policemen and Port Sunlight firemen wearing their ceremonial brass helmets. A group on top of the offices have a bird's eye view of the proceedings*

Above: *Monkey Brand department workers pose for the photographer, George Davies, in eager anticipation of the Royal Party's tour of the factory*

Above: *The west wing of the offices have a more formal decoration than the factory in readiness for the visit of the King & Queen*

Above: *The King accompanied by Sir William Lever descends the stairs in No.3 Packing Room to meet another group of workers, while the rest of the Royal Party follow behind*

Above: *This department, as well as all the others throughout the factory, were gaily decorated in preparation for the Royal Party[PRG]*

Above: *The workers bid farewell as the Royal Party leaves the factory*

Above: *The workers on the left and officials on the right are waiting for the official laying of the foundation stone of the Lady Lever Art Gallery. It was laid by remote control by their Majesties from Hulme Hall using a small model of the stone and crane. The white building in the background on Greendale Road was later demolished and the two buildings behind the men on the left (Nos.2 & 4 Windy Bank) were later moved to their present position. This was done to improve the view of the Art Gallery from Greendale Road and the Birkenhead to Chester railway which can be seen in the background*[PRG]

Above: *The dancers have stopped to pose for this photograph at Port Sunlight taken on 21 April 1914 at what was described as a 'Royal Dance' held in the Auditorium*

Below: *In contrast to the pageantry of the Royal Visit, this was one of a series of photographs taken by George Davies in New Chester Road of 'The Pals' on their way to Hooton Training Camp on 23 September 1914. According to the message on the back of one which was sent from Hooton Camp, the pictures were later sold to the recruits as postcards*

SHELL-MAKING, AND DISCOVERY OF A NEW GAS

In response to a request from Mr. Lloyd George's Government, in the autumn of 1915, Lever Brothers Limited undertook to make shells. The available plant for repair work at Port Sunlight was immediately utilized, fresh machinery was made, and the necessary gauges for the shells were constructed by the firm itself. The difficulty of obtaining special tools was also overcome by their being made at Port Sunlight. On October 25th, 1915, the first delivery of shells was made, and from then until the end of June, 1916, when the Government intimated that they had sufficient for their purpose, the average weekly number of shells delivered was 320, making a total of nearly 12,000. The percentage of rejected shells was only 1.6 which at that time was considered a record, and even that small percentage was principally due to faulty material. Owing to the withdrawal of men for military service, and to the necessity of keeping the remainder of their plant at work on urgent repair, the Company were compelled, in order to reach the maximum shell output, to train youths and unskilled men in the use of machine tools— a training which was attended with satisfactory results. Experiments in gas warfare were undertaken by members of Lever Brothers' research laboratory staff, with the result that a gas was discovered which was used before the present mustard gas, and arrangements were made by the Military Authorities for its production on a large scale. The gas proved quite satisfactory, and the substance was afterwards known at the front as " PS"

Below: This article appeared in the Birkenhead News Victory Souvenir book

Above: The caption for this postcard posted in 1915 read: "The Club & Bowling Green, Port Sunlight". On the left, the original building still with its domed roof, on the right the extension opened in 1910

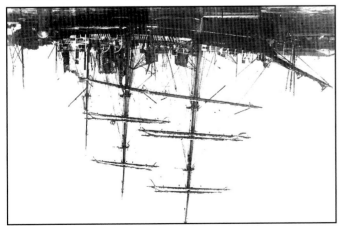

Above: The Lever Brother's barque Sunlight was launched in 1907. On 6 June 1915 she was sunk by a German submarine with all 20 crew being saved by a Government trawler PRG

Jan 6	A preliminary muster of the Port Sunlight Volunteer Training Corps was held in the Auditorium with Sir William Lever the first to sign. He insisted on taking his place in the ranks as a Private
May 20	Saddle tank locomotive *Queen Mary* delivered new to the factory
Jun 6	Lever Brothers' barque *Sunlight* was torpedoed and sunk - no casualties (*see photo*)
Jun 28	Sir William Lever addressed a mass meeting of employees in the Auditorium to discuss the war situation - he said the company was very proud of its men who had answered the nation's call, but went on to say there were other ways for everyone to help the war effort – namely money in the form of War Loans
Jul 1	Birth of Philip William Bryce Lever - later to become the 3rd Lord Leverhulme
Jul 31	Port Sunlight Company of the Birkenhead Battalion of the Cheshire Volunteer Regiment attended a camp at Rivington, near Bolton, on land owned by Sir William Lever
Aug 8	Philip William Bryce Lever was baptised at Christ Church Port Sunlight
Aug 14	The gold cross of the 'Port Sunlight Order of Conspicuous Merit' was awarded to 17 year-old Samuel Cooper for rescuing a 7 year-old boy from drowning in a canal at Bank Hall
Sep	Sir William Lever became Honorary Treasurer of the 'Star & Garter Home for the Disabled Soldiers, Sailors and Airmen' at Richmond
Oct	Two separate communications were received from the front using *Sunlight Soap* cartons as postcards - they were ultimately to be placed with other 'war curios' in the Hulme Hall Art Gallery and Museum
Oct 3	The Park Road Schools were given a new name by Sir William Lever – the 'Lyceum' which was to become the headquarters of the Sunday School, the Boys' Brigade, prospective companies of Boy Scouts and Girl Guides as well as other clubs and institutions
Oct 23	A silver Loving Cup was presented to baby Philip Lever by the tenant farmers of the Leverhulme Estate
Oct 25	First delivery made of shells produced at Port Sunlight to help the war effort (*see article on this page*)
Nov	Port Sunlight Girl Guides started

Below: The 'Pals' from Port Sunlight with the 18th King's Liverpool Regiment are pictured on 29 April 1915 before leaving Knowsley Camp for Brigade training at Grantham PRG

1916

Above: On 15 January 1915 Lieut.-Col. MC Ellis VD, the Birkenhead Battalion Commandant, opened the new 25 yard Miniature Rifle Range at Port Sunlight which was supplied by Lever Brothers. Afterwards the visitors retired to Hulme Hall for tea PRG

Above: The Port Sunlight Ambulance Brigade are seen at Thornton Manor where The Hon WH and Mrs Lever equipped a Red Cross Hospital which was maintained throughout the war until January 1919

Above: Following a storm on New Year's Day 1916, a building on the Bebington Showground [now the Oval] collapsed on the 2nd Garrison Battalion of the Cheshires, killing one of their men. The troops were then billeted in the Auditorium, Port Sunlight, which meant the Volunteers already stationed there had to relocate their headquarters to the smaller Gladstone Hall. The soldiers of the Cheshires can be seen in their new surroundings of the Auditorium still decorated for Christmas festivities PRG

employees on active service or prisoners of war by the Chairman, Directors, staff and employees of Lever Brothers
— Planters Margarine Works erected
— Port Sunlight Badminton Club formed – 22 members

1916

Jan 1 A storm blew down a building on the Bebington Showground where the 2nd Garrison Battalion of the Cheshires were stationed - a number of troops had to be billeted in the Auditorium with the Volunteers having to transfer their headquarters to Gladstone Hall *(see photo)*

Jan 15 A new 25 yard Miniature Rifle Range at Port Sunlight, paid for by Lever Brothers, was opened by Lieut.-Col. MC Ellis, the Battalion Commander

Feb 12 The Port Sunlight Company of the Birkenhead Battalion, Volunteer Training Corps held a Field Day - they were asked by the Police authorities to co-operate with them in the event of enemy air attacks *(see photo)*

Mar 16 It was announced that up to this date 2,158 employees of Lever Brothers Limited, from Head and Branch Offices, and the Works, were on active service. Of these 65 had been killed in action or died of wounds; 5 missing; 7 prisoners of war; 96 wounded or invalided on active service without being discharged and 286 had been discharged

Mar 30 Announced at AGM – 3,451 employees now in the Services

Apr The Hon WH and Mrs Lever equipped a Red Cross Hospital at Thornton Manor – after the furniture etc had being moved into storage at Hulme Hall – the first patients were admitted in July *(see photo)*

Apr 7 The Port Sunlight Girl Guides were enrolled as a 40-strong Company by Miss Royden, County Commissioner - there were 20 recruits on probation

Apr 13 The Progress Club was opened by Sir William Lever in premises above the Lever Free Library, previously occupied by the Boys' Brigade

Apr 29 Bromboro Port Steam Ship Company formed

May 21 The 'Summer Time' Act launched which advanced the clocks by one hour resulting in fuel economies

Jun Lever Brothers purchased quarries at Gwernymynydd, near Mold, North Wales to quarry silicate suitable for producing *Monkey Brand & Vim*

Jun 11 A Memorial Service was held in the Auditorium for Field-Marshal the Earl Kitchener who was drowned following the sinking of HMS *Hampshire* off the Orkneys on 5 June 1916

Jul 6 The first patients admitted to the Thornton Hough Red Cross Hospital at *Thornton Manor* were from the Somme offensive. Sir William Lever had placed the Ball Room, Music Room and a few other rooms at *Thornton Manor* in the hands of the Thornton Hough Red Cross to equip and staff it. It was maintained through to January 1919 with the Port Sunlight Ambulance Section providing night orderlies for the hospital

Jul 21/22 Last of the 1916 annual children's treats when the Chairman's motor cars and Thornton Manor motor omnibuses transported them to *Thornton Manor.* Soon after, petrol restrictions were introduced which curtailed such pleasures

Aug 2 Purchase of Bebington Show Ground for use as a recreation ground when released by the War Office

Oct 12 Saddle tank locomotive *Prince of Wales* delivered to Port Sunlight

Dec For the third year Christmas parcels sent to all

Above: This illustration of Lord Leverhulme's Coat of Arms, granted to him when he became Baron Leverhulme of Bolton-le-Moors, appeared in Port Sunlight's house magazine Progress. The Latin motto means "I scorn to change or fear." PPRG

Right: This was a poster advertisement featured in the Port Sunlight magazine Progress when Lieut. EV Salaman requested "the pleasure of your company" at the No.9 Platoon of the 2nd Battalion Cheshire Volunteer Regiment's Hot Pot Parade on 24 October 1917 at the Co-Partners' Club PPRG

Mar 22 A Blind Musicians' Concert for blinded soldiers and sailors was given at the Auditorium in aid of the St Dunstan's Hostel For The Blind in London

Mar 25 At the morning service in Christ Church, Port Sunlight, a silver cross and 2 silver flower vases were placed on the Communion Table – being a gift of Hon. Mr & Mrs WH Lever to commemorate the baptism of their son Philip William Bryce Lever on 8 August 1915

Apr Joseph Watson sold his shares in the Soapmakers Watson & Sons to Lever Brothers for £800,000. Lever Brothers taking complete control in 1921

May 15 Over 100 members of 'C' Company the 2nd Battalion of the Cheshire Volunteer Regiment from Port Sunlight lined up on St George's Hall Plateau in Liverpool to welcome their Majesties King George V and Queen Mary

Jun 15 Captain the Hon. W Hulme Lever (2nd Battalion of the Cheshire Volunteer Regiment Port Sunlight) inspected the Boys' Brigade at their Annual Inspection and Prize distribution in the Auditorium

Jun 21 Sir William Hesketh Lever raised to the Peerage when he was created Baron Leverhulme of Bolton-le-Moors (see photo)

Jun 29 The Chairman, now Lord Leverhulme, completed 50 years of business life

Jul 13 The third locomotive to bear the name *Sydney* was purchased second-hand – scrapped in 1922

Jul 24 Lord Leverhulme took the oath and his seat in the House of Lords

Sep The Royal National Eisteddfod of Wales was held in Birkenhead – Lord Leverhulme acted as president

Sep 8 Tour of the Village and Factory by Prime Minister Rt Hon Lloyd George & his wife who made a visit to Port Sunlight after visiting the Welsh Eisteddfod in Birkenhead – they stayed as guests of Lord Leverhulme at *Thornton Manor* for 4 nights

Sep 20 The 9th annual distribution of Co-Partnership Certificates was held in the Auditorium

Oct 24 No 9 Platoon of the 2nd Battalion Volunteer Regiment held their annual 'Hot Pot Parade' and Smoking Concert at the Co-Partners' Club

— A book entitled *Port Sunlight* by Mr T Raffles Davison was published – it was a record of the village's artistic and pictorial aspect – cost five shillings

— Winter Port Sunlight Girls' Sewing Party sent 250 shirts and 200 pairs of socks to three Cheshire Battalions

— Lord Leverhulme was appointed as High Sheriff of the County Palatine of Lancaster for 1917-18

— Lever Brothers Staff Training College started in former Park Road Schools, renamed the Lyceum in 1915

Jan 2	Lord Leverhulme's son, the Hon. W Hulme Lever, was made Acting-Chairman of Lever Brothers
Feb 1	A Serbian Commercial and Industrial Mission Limited visited Port Sunlight during the course of their tour of the United Kingdom – arranged by the new Government Department of Overseas Trade which linked the Foreign Office with the Board of Trade
Feb 23	Death of Lord Leverhulme's sister, Mary Tillotson, whose son, John Lever Tillotson, was a Director of Lever Brothers
Feb 27	First of 3 Welsh Flag Days at Port Sunlight which raised £519. 6 shillings
Mar 2	The Flag Week Closing Concert proved so popular that the venue had to be changed from the Lyceum to The Auditorium
Mar 4	The start of Aeroplane Week during which aeroplanes from Hooton Aerodrome flew over the works and village scattering leaflets (see copy of poster)
Apr	Sanitas & Co Ltd - disinfectant manufacturers of London taken over by Lever Brothers
Jun 1	Fire broke out at No. 1 Oil Mill but due to the prompt action of the Port Sunlight Brigade the fire was brought under control in 3 hours
Jun 4	Lord Leverhulme's maiden speech in the House of Lords was in moving the rejection of Lord Southwark's Coinage (Decimal System) Bill - he was not opposed to Decimal Coinage but he objected to the Bill's proposal to 'dethrone the British penny'. Following this Lord Leverhulme was appointed a Royal Commissioner on Decimal Coinage
Jul 4	Lever Brothers Transport Company - SPD (Speedy Prompt Delivery) - formed
Jul 6	Port Sunlight welcomed United States soldiers and sailors who played an exhibition game of baseball on the Pool Bank Football ground which was followed by a game of football between 2 teams of Port Sunlight workgirls
Aug	Lord Leverhulme became Mayor of his native town Bolton for 1918-19 (see photo opposite)
Nov	A silver statuette of an infantryman was presented to Lever Brothers "in recognition of their close association with and keen interest in the 13th Service Battalion, The Cheshire Regiment" by the survivors of the unit
Nov 11	**Armistice Day – 1st World War ended**
Nov 28	*Prince Albert*, first Saddle tank locomotive with a back cab, delivered new
Dec	Saddle tank locomotive *Prince John* delivered, twin to *Prince Albert*
—	*Planter*, the only fireless locomotive known to have operated on the Lever Brothers railway system, was used at the Planters Margarine Works
—	Saddle tank locomotive *Lux* delivered to Port Sunlight (former locomotive *Lux* renamed *Princess Mary*)
—	Both Hulme Hall and the Lyceum were used as Military Hospitals, as well as the Port Sunlight Cottage Hospital

Above: This poster was displayed throughout Port Sunlight Village and the works which explained the Government's Aeroplane Week which operated from 4-9 March during which aeroplanes from Hooton Aerodrome flew over the works and village scattering leaflets "A message from the clouds" inviting subscriptions for the cause.
During the week, over £183,433 was raised in National War Bonds - enough for over 70 aeroplanes

Comic Postcard with a soap theme - posted in 1918

Feb 12	*Australia,* first of 3 side tank steam locomotives to be delivered to Port Sunlight
Mar	*Canada & India* side tank locomotives delivered to Port Sunlight
Apr 23	Birth of Rosemary Gertrude Lever, second daughter of The Hon. & Mrs William Hulme Lever
Apr 24	A 'Welcome Home Dinner' followed by a concert in the Auditorium was given to the men who had returned home from war, together with their wives
Jul	Lord Leverhulme elected President of a new Association for the Advancement of Education in Industry and Commerce
Jul 19	Recreation Ground for employees opened at Bebington [formerly the site of the Wirral & Birkenhead Agricultural Society and now the Oval] with a 'Celebration of Peace' (*see photo next page*)
Aug 1	The 1st Port Sunlight Boys' Brigade camp held on land at Thurstaston - recently acquired by Lever Brothers to establish a company holiday camp (now a caravan park)
Aug 8	A Fancy Dress Victory Ball held at the Auditorium
Sep	Southern Whaling & Sealing Co Ltd taken over by Lever Brothers
Sep	Lever Brothers purchased 50% share in the Thames Paper Co Ltd, makers of 'Fiberite' fibreboard cases which untimately replaced the traditional wooden soap boxes used to pack soap tablets
Sep 24	Bus service between New Ferry, Thornton Hough & Heswall started – appreciated by Lever employees
Sep 27	Railway Strike began - Lever Brothers agreed to loan 15 four-ton motor wagons to help the collection of milk churns from North Wales (*see photos*)
Oct 6	Railway Strike ends during which time Lever Brothers' motors ran 7,715 miles and delivered 2,989 churns of milk for the Food Controller (*see photo*)
Oct 8	Lever Brothers Limited took over Crosfields of Warrington and Gossages of Widnes
Oct 8	Rev Ralph WT Middleton inducted as the new Pastor at Christ Church Port Sunlight
Oct 24	Lever Brothers took over Prices' Patent Candle Co Ltd, candle manufacturers of Battersea & Bromborough Pool
Nov 11	At 11am a 2 minutes silence was observed throughout Lever Brothers' Offices & Works as a mark of respect for those who fell in the 'Great War'
Nov 12	Co-Partners Club War Memorial unveiled - Lord Leverhulme presented gold watches bearing suitable inscriptions to employees who had gained military distinction in the recent war
Nov 28	Wages first paid directly into Lever Brothers employees' bank accounts for those requesting the new system instead of traditional cash
Dec	Bromborough Port Construction Co Ltd formed out of the former building department of Lever Brothers
—	Work started on construction of a building for packaging Vinolia products on the corner of Quarry Road and Bromborough Road (now the site of Unilever Research)
—	Model for proposed War Memorial exhibited at the Royal Academy

Left: *Seen here in his chain of office, Lord Leverhulme's final council meeting as Mayor of his native Bolton was on 22 October 1919. His daughter-in-law, wife of the Hon. William Hulme Lever, acted as his Mayoress*

Above: *Milk churns are being unloaded from a Lever Brothers' wagon during the railway strike from 27 September to 6 October. Lever Brothers agreed to loan 15 four-ton motor wagons to help the Birkenhead Food Committee collection of milk churns from the North Wales district during which time their motors ran 7,715 miles and delivered 2,989 churns of milk*[PRG]

Below: *Lever Brothers' factory girls are seen in New Chester Road being transported by horse & cart from work during the strike when trams were unable to cope with the extra passengers*[PRG]

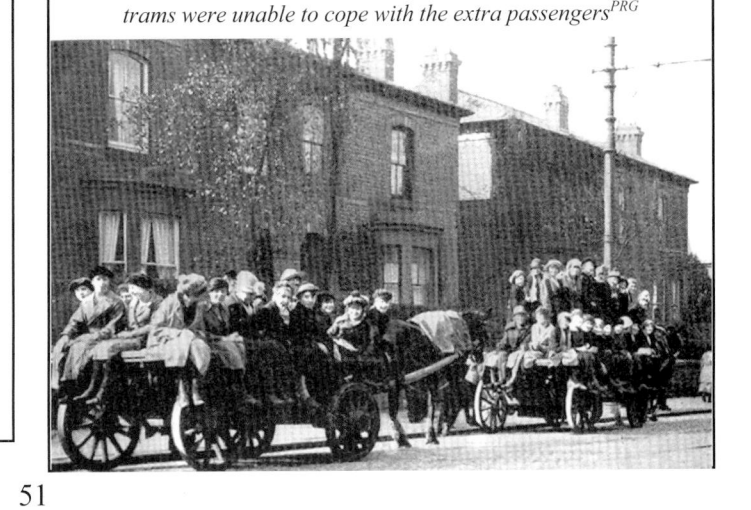

Above: *In 1919, Lever Brothers invited the Manchester and District Bank to occupy part of these premises in Greendale Road. Seen here they occupied the left end, whilst the Levers' Savings Bank, whose sign can be seen in the window, were in the right-hand end. Upstairs were the library and a clubroom*

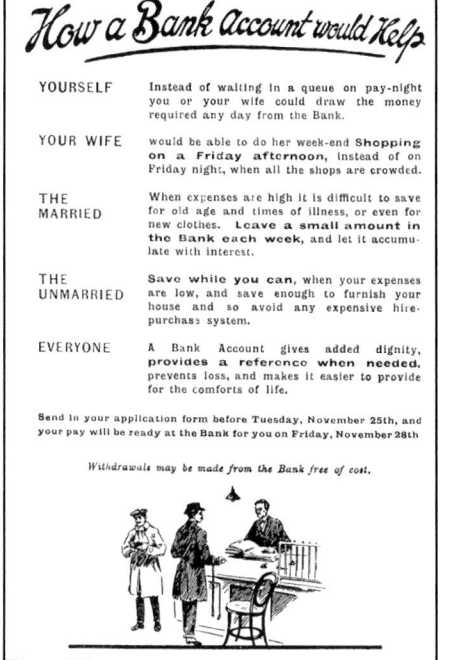

Following Lever Brothers invitation to the Manchester & District Banking Company Limited to occupy premises in Greendale Road the Company encouraged employees to open bank accounts and have their pay credited direct to the bank. The company produced posters and also featured this information in a 1919 edition of Progress[PRG]

Above: *In 1919 the former grounds of the Wirral & Birkenhead Agricultural Society re-opened as the Port Sunlight Recreation Ground (the Oval) seen here, the large wooden stand was more recently featured in the filming of* Chariots of Fire

Right: *On 13 November Mrs Graham the Manageress of Lever's Dining Room extinguished the flames from a chip pan which set alight the clothes worn by one of the kitchen maids. For her act of bravery she was awarded the first ever Gallant Conduct award by the British Industrial Safety First Association. She was also awarded 'The Port Sunlight Order of Conspicuous Merit' which was regularly presented to members of the Port Sunlight community who performed acts of bravery*[PRG]

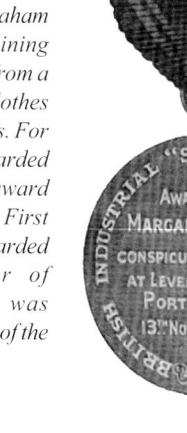

Above: *Work began in 1919 on the construction of the building in the centre foreground for packaging* Vinolia *products. On the corner of Quarry Road and Bromborough Road, the site is now occupied by Unilever Research*

Above: *The Reverend Ralph Middleton took over as Minister of Christ Church in October 1919*

Feb 2	Lever Brothers bought an additional 85 acres of land adjoining Higher Bebington Road for the extension of the recreation areas already purchased from the Bebington Show Grounds
Mar 3	Bebington Athletic & General Stores Ltd opened – sports outfitters in connection with Port Sunlight Recreation Association
Mar 8	Access to the Port Sunlight private railway halt was extended with subways driven under the railway through the back of the former Concert Hall
Mar 12	Lord Leverhulme departed for a visit to South Africa aboard the RMS *Llanstephan Castle* with a party including his son the Hon WH Lever
Apr 1	Lever Brothers' Dental Surgery started
May	Lord Leverhulme's first flight in an aeroplane from Paris to London (*see photo*)
May 13	Inter-union dispute at Lever Brothers leads to a 3-week strike of clerical staff
Jun 19	The 1st and 2nd Companies of the Port Sunlight Girl Guides, joined by the Bebington Girl Guides, held their camp for a week at *Thornton Manor* by kind permission of The Hon.Mrs William Hulme Lever (District Commissioner) (*see photo*)
Jul	Lever Brothers acquired a controlling interest , via their subsidiary Crosfields, in J & E Atkinson Ltd - perfumers and soapmakers of London
Jul 13	Despite opposition by the Mersey Docks and Harbour Board and the Manchester Ship Canal Company, the Bill enabling Lever Brothers to develop Bromborough Dock became an Act of Parliament
Jul 31	The 1st Port Sunlight Boys' Brigade attended a weeks' camp on the Leverhulme Estate at Thurstaston (now the caravan park)
Aug 3	Vinolia department opened on the site on Quarry Road now occupied by Unilever Research
Aug 4	Lever Brothers' Motor Ambulance arrived
Sep	The 6.25 acres 'Warren' sports field at Eastham rented to the Planters Margarine Company's Sports Club (now Leverhulme Playing Fields)
Sep 13	Re-launch *of Twink* – a soap dye in the form of fine flakes, available in up to 24 different shades, which combined the functions of washing and dyeing various fabrics into a single operation
Oct	Port Sunlight Orchestra re-formed – a revival of the old organisation which had been disbanded during the war
Oct	It was decided by a Joint Committee of the two houses of Parliament that Port Sunlight and Bromborough would not be absorbed by Birkenhead
Oct	There were 9 football and 2 hockey teams in Port Sunlight Village and 2 football pitches at the Recreation Ground
—	The headquarters of the Port Sunlight Boys' Brigade was transferred to the new Recreation Ground

Right: View inside the Vestibule of the General Offices showing the pictures and model of the village which were displayed here for the benefit of visitors[PRG]

Above: *This picture, taken from the front of Lord Leverhulme's Christmas Card of 1920 shows him about to climb aboard his first ever flight which transported him from Paris to London*

Above: *The Port Sunlight and Bebington Girl Guides in camp at Thornton Manor*[PRG]

Right: *A Vim*[UNI] *advert from the time*

Above: *The competitors are ready for the 'off' at an athletics meeting being held at the Port Sunlight Recreation Ground*[PRG]

Above: *Seen here in 1921, the 1st team of the Port Sunlight Rugby Football Club, still known then as the 'Cosmopolitans' to the outside world*

Right: *In this view of the factory, part of the extensive rail network inside the works can be clearly seen. On the right is No.4 factory, on the left the River Dibbin, with the New Chester Road beyond*

Above: *An aerial view of the factory taken in 1920. In the distance the River Mersey, in the centre the factory and village, and on the right the completed Vinolia works*

Below: *Another aerial photograph taken in 1920 shows the Birkenhead to Chester railway line in the foreground, the New Chester Road running parallel to it in the background with Port Sunlight Village and Works in between. Wharf Island and Port Sunlight Dock are to the left of the works, whilst Christ Church and the Auditorium can be seen in the centre of the village*

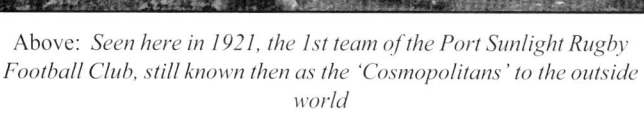

THURSTASTON CAMP.

In connection with the re-opening of the above Camp, the following poster has been displayed in the Port Sunlight Offices :—

LEVER BROTHERS LIMITED
EMPLOYEES'
HOLIDAY AND WEEK-END CAMP
AT
THURSTASTON.

Opening and Closing Dates. 1. The Camp will be open for the accommodation of members of the Port Sunlight Recreations Association from 1st June until June 30th September, 1921.

Accommodation. 2. The accommodation provided will consist of :-
(a) Bed, blankets, sheets, pillows and cases and lockers, in a sleeping hut which accommodates 10 persons.
(b) The use of the washing facilities, etc., in the lavatory huts.
(c) The use of tables, forms and chairs in the dining hut.
(d) The use of a fire upon which simple meals may be cooked.
(e) A limited supply of hot water.
(f) Facilities for the practice of Football, Cricket, Rounders, Basket Ball, etc.

Members should therefore take with them to the Camp such food, crockery, cutlery, cooking utensils and soap, towels, etc., which they will require during their stay. Additional supplies may be obtained at West Kirby (3 miles distant).

Arrangements will be made to enable Campers to obtain, on the premises, a limited number of articles, such as tins of sardines, biscuits, lemonade, etc., also bicycle repair outfits, etc., at shop prices.

Charges. 3. The charges for accommodation will be:-
For Adults - - 1/- per night or 5/- per week
For Juniors (under 14) 9d. " " " 3/9 "

Procedure. 4. Members who desire to stay in the Camp must send in an application to the Recreations Office, so as to reach it at least 3 days beforehand. This application will be returned and, if "approved," should be handed into the Time Office for the Works, and the Cash Office for the Offices, with the amount covering the charges for the whole period of the visit. Application forms can be obtained from the Time Office or Cash Office.

The application "approved" and receipted by the Cashier, will be the Voucher for the accommodation in the Camp, and must be handed to the Camp Caretaker on arrival.

Members who wish to prolong their stay must give notice to the Camp Caretaker at least 2 days beforehand, and, should accommodation be available, pay the covering charges in advance.

Limit of Accommodation. 5. Accommodation in the Camp is limited to :-
East Wing - - - Ladies 60
West Wing - - - Men 90

Parties. 6. Several members wishing to proceed to the Camp in one party should send in one application to cover the whole party to obtain accommodation as such

Day Visitors. 7. On application to the Camp Caretaker, day visitors may obtain tion of their Membership Cards, if available.

Means of Access. 8. The Camp can be reached by Motor 'Bus from Birkenhead and New Ferry, by Train from Rock Ferry and Birkenhead to Thurstaston. See local Time Tables.

LEVER BROTHERS LIMITED.
30th May, 1921.

Left: Pictured at Pool Bank ground are the Port Sunlight Juniors with their trophies and medals gained in the 1920/21 season:-
Back Row Lt. to Rt. Secretary A Malinson, T Newby, C Millington, W Butler, A Whitehead, J Williams and trainer Joe Williams
Centre: J Wallace, A Roberts, G Edge, and G Davies
Front: E Sweeney, and E Brown[PRG]

Above: The very popular Thurstaston Camp was situated on the easterly bank of the Dee Estuary facing across to the rising Welsh hills. There were spacious grounds surrounding the well-equipped army huts which housed the campers: 90 in the men's wing and 60 in the ladies'. Charges for Juniors: one shilling per night or five shillings per week; for Juniors (under 14) Nine pence per night or three shillings and nine pence per week [19p][PRG]

Below: Children from the Charles Thompson Mission are enjoying themselves on see-saws at Thurstaston Camp

---

Feb 23 New Leyland No.2 Motor Fire Engine brought into service – Port Sunlight now had 2 of the most modern fire engines and the latest motor ambulances all manned by 17 full-time officers and men – the old horse-drawn Fire Engine was repainted and offered to Stornoway Town Council *(see photos next page)*

Mar 12 Bus route commenced from Rock Ferry Pier, running through Woodhey to Port Sunlight

Apr 8 A partial eclipse of the sun was seen at Port Sunlight

Apr 23 Lord Leverhulme unveiled the Thornton Hough War Memorial

May 5 Lord Leverhulme again travelled by air - this time from Hendon to Paris

May 19 The Bebington Show Grounds Ltd (former occupiers of the Recreation Ground) was officially wound up

May 25 First baby born at Bromborough Pool Maternity Home was Irene Charlotte Marsh

Jun 1 Holiday Camp for Lever employees re-opened at Thurstaston *(see poster)* [still there - now the Thurstaston Caravan Park]

Sep 10 The recently formed 13th Cheshire Comrades Association visited Lord Leverhulme's home at Rivington near Bolton

Oct The Village Dental Clinic was opened at 22 Bolton Road

Dec 2 A cordial welcome was given to 800 new Co-Partners present at a meeting in the Auditorium

Dec 3 The Port Sunlight War Memorial was unveiled by an ex-service man, chosen by ballot, in memory of the 481 Port Sunlight men who fell in the war *(see photos next page)*

Dec 3 The Port Sunlight branch of the Royal British Legion was formed

— Lever Brothers' Head Office moved to London

— New roads built on Shore Drive Estate - between New Chester Road and the river with 123 houses and 4 shops

— Port Sunlight Athletic Club formed - training Monday, Wednesday and Friday evenings

— Central Power Station built on the banks of the Mersey to supply electricity to Lever Brothers and its subsidiary companies in the area

Above: *Seen outside the Gymnasium, the new motorised fire engine was delivered to Port Sunlight in February 1921*[PSN]

Above: *Standing in the centre of Port Sunlight Village on the former site of the Gymnasium, the War Memorial was officially unveiled by Sergeant TG (Mo) Eames on 3 December 1921 assisted by Private Cruikshank VC and Lord Leverhulme. The memorial was designed by Sir W Goscombe John RA. It is dominated by a granite village cross surrounded by 11 bronze figures symbolising the 'defence of the home'. The parapet surrounding the platform carries four bronze groups representing the Sea, Land and Air Forces and the Red Cross. Eight panels on either side of the steps depict boys and girls' offering garlands in token of the gratitude of the generations to come for the sacrifice which made sure of their heritage'*

Above: *With the arrival of a second motor fire engine at Port Sunlight, the horse-drawn engine became superfluous, so Lord Leverhulme offered it the the Town Council of Stornaway in Scotland and it was gratefully accepted. It is seen here outside Lever Brothers' main offices with the newly painted Stornaway arms and lettering*[PSN]

Below: *The unveiling ceremony*

Above: *The new Humber motor ambulance for Lever Brothers was delivered to Port Sunlight and was featured in the Levers' magazine* Progress. *It described the livery as 'dark green picked out with gilt and green lines with the inside finished in white '*[PSN]

Mar		Mac Fisheries Ltd (including their subsidiary T Wall & Sons Ltd) taken over by Lever Brothers from Lord Leverhulme
Jul	22	Unemployment, Sickness and Death Benefit Scheme and the linked bonus system introduced. A new housing scheme on the Storeton Estate was outlined by Lord Leverhulme including a mortgage scheme to help buyers
Jul	27	Lever Brothers introduced Group Life Insurance and unemployment half pay and sickness half-pay schemes
Aug	27	The King's Colours of the 13th (Wirral) Battalion, The Cheshire Regiment was transferred to Christ Church Port Sunlight and a Memorial Tablet unveiled (*see photo*)
Aug	31	Leverhulme Masonic Lodge consecrated at the Lady Lever Art Gallery (*see photo*)
Sep	21	New Works Employees' Advisory Committee elected
Nov	18	First issue of *Port Sunlight News*
Nov	27	William Lever created 'Viscount Leverhulme of the Western Isles' - his name being amongst those submitted to King George by the Prime Minister on the resignation of the Coalition Government
Dec	16	Lady Lever Art Gallery opened by HRH Princess Beatrice (*see photos*)
—		Due to an increasing demand for water at Port Sunlight an Artesian Well was drilled to a depth of 550 ft. outside No1 Power House in the Factory. It was expected to produce 45,000 gallons of pure water each hour
—		Saddle tank locomotive *Mersey* purchased about this time

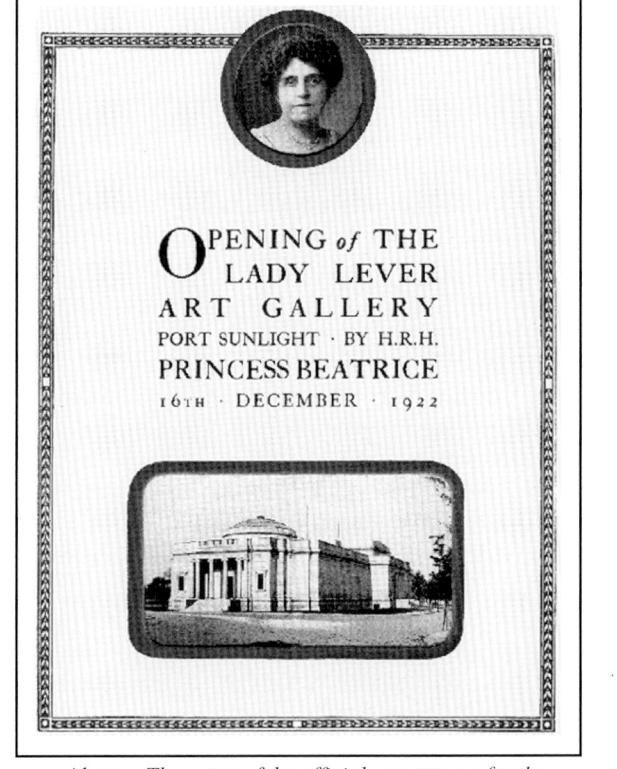

Above: *The cover of the official programme for the opening of the Lady Lever Gallery*

On Saturday 16 December 1922 the Lady Lever Art Gallery was officially opened by HRH Princess Beatrice, the youngest daughter of the late Queen Victoria (*pictured right*)

Below:
The Art Gallery from the South

Left:
Lord Leverhulme carrying the King's Colours of the 13th Battalion of the Cheshire Regiment into Christ Church, Port Sunlight where it still hangs today[PSN]

Right: *Seen here with Lord Leverhulme after its consecration on 31 August 1922, the officers of Leverhulme Masonic Lodge No. 4438 Back row: Bros. HL Armstrong, JG Tyrell and GRN Tremayne Second Row: Bros. J Knox, NL Lythgoe, ER Ellis, H Wilkinson, A Davies, J Darcy Lever and F Statham Front row: Bros. W Wainwright, CW Barnish, J Wainwright, C Walton and Lord Leverhulme*[PSN]

1923

Feb — Zog Ltd - soapmakers and cleansers - taken over by Lever Brothers

Feb 6 — Captain Bruce Bairnsfather, whose *Fragments From France* cheered the nation during the war, paid a visit to Port Sunlight

Mar — Through the generosity of the Company a wireless receiving set was installed by the Port Sunlight Radio Club in the Lyceum - members were able to 'listen-in' to concerts held in Manchester

Apr 7 — Lever Brothers presented new headquarters at Port Sunlight Recreation Ground to the Port Sunlight Company of Territorials - 'D' Company 4/5 Battalion of the Cheshire Regiment - it included a drill hall, miniature rifle range, company orderly room and mess rooms *(see photo)*

Apr 11 — Hobbies Show opened at Hulme Hall by the Marquess of Carisbrooke

May 5 — Port Sunlight AFC won the Wirral Amateur Cup at Hoylake by beating Heswall AFC 4-2

May 23-24 — Gala Weekend at Thurstaston Camp enjoyed by over 250 employees

Jul — Since the Lady Lever Art Gallery opened 7 months previously over 100,000 visitors were recorded

Jul 5 — Last of the visitors to Port Sunlight in connection with the centenary of the apprenticeship to the grocery trade of the late Mr James Lever

Jul 6 — Art Gallery ownership transferred from Viscount Leverhulme to Trustees

Jul — Angus Watson & Co Ltd - in the fishing industry - taken over by Lever Brothers

Aug — Complaints were made against unsightly buildings on the allotments and owners were asked by the Estate Department to give reasons why they should not be removed and if there were no good reasons they should be replaced or removed

Aug — Lever Brothers' Ophthalmic clinic started

Aug 1 — Port Sunlight 'Front Garden Competition' started

Sep 19 — On his 72nd birthday Lord Leverhulme formally announced a scheme for building on the Edgeworth Estate between the Works and Spital Station with freehold plots being offered gratis. The householders could design their property and employ their own builder providing the standard was approved by the company's Architect. Preference was given to Co-Partners and there were Government subsidies available

Sep 29/30 — Closing Carnival for the season at Thurstaston Camp which was attended by the Hon W Hulme & Mrs Lever

Oct 6 — The Port Sunlight Operatic and Drama Society performed the play *Pan from the Past* which had been written by the Hon WH Lever under the pseudonym 'William Thornton'

Oct 8 — First meeting of the newly formed Port Sunlight Lecture Society at the Lyceum when the Hon WH Lever gave a lecture entitled *Nigeria*

Nov 14 — Lord Leverhulme started the first leg of his 5th round-the-world trip

Nov 21 — Port Sunlight Arts Club's inauguration of their new club room in Hulme Hall

1923

Above: The Port Sunlight Company of Territorials – 'D' Company, 4/5 Battalion, the Cheshire Regiment, are officially taking command of their new Headquarters at the Port Sunlight Recreation Ground on 7 April 1923. Presented by Lever Brothers Ltd, the accommodation included: a company orderly room, drill hall, miniature rifle range, mess rooms and "everything requisite to the service and domestic economy of a military unit" PSN

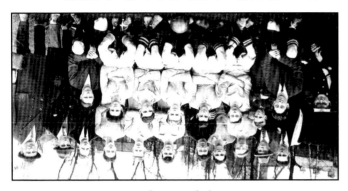

Above: Christ Church AFC with their officials 1922/23 season

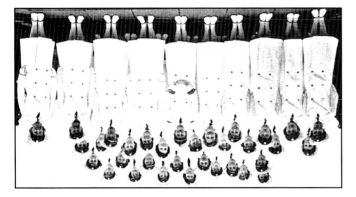

Above: The 1923 Port Sunlight in-house magazine Progress describes these girls as "a corps of engagingly-uniformed Lady Guides … the pretty girls of Port Sunlight" PRG

— St John's Ambulance Brigade re-formed – disbanded during the war as most of its members had joined the armed forces

— Port Sunlight Golf Association formed

— Over 4,000 visitors enjoyed the 2-day 'Hobbies and Crafts' exhibition held at Hulme Hall - Lord Leverhulme declared "the pursuit of hobbies was one of the greatest joys of life and within the reach of everyone"

— A corps of engagingly-uniformed lady guides known as 'the pretty girls from Port Sunlight' conducted visitors round the factory and village *(see photo)*

Mar 6 The tall brickworks' chimney on the river bank near New Ferry was demolished

Mar 27 Lord Leverhulme returned to Port Sunlight after a 40,000 mile world tour of Lever Brothers' interests

Jun 30 First employees' excursion to the British Empire Exhibition at Wembley

Jul 28 The last of 5 employees' excursions to London for the British Empire Exhibition

Oct 10 The 'All Blacks' New Zealand Rugby team visited Port Sunlight prior to playing Cheshire at Birkenhead Park

Nov For only the second time, the Port Sunlight Horticultural Society included a Chrysanthemum Show together with flowers, vegetables and over 200 homing pigeons

Dec In 1924 there were over 80,000 visitors to the Port Sunlight factory and village from all over the world

Dec Anti-waste campaign at the Port Sunlight factory

Dec 6 Official opening of *Dunfield* the first house completed on the Edgeworth Estate (*see photo*)

— Employees' Office Advisory Committee formed

— Commissioning of the Calcining and Grinding Plant, where rocks were ground into small particles for use in scouring products such as *Vim*

— Windy Bank houses demolished to be rebuilt and open up the west vista of the Art Gallery

JUST FANCY! WHEN WE STARTED AN HOUR AGO, WE WERE ALL PERFECT STRANGERS TO EACH OTHER!

Above: *Lever Brothers' Management decided that due to 'shoals' of humorous postcards, similar to this 1920s postcard, being sent to the factory, all personal correspondence and communications must be sent to home addresses*

Above: *The arrivals at Levers' Thurstaston Holiday Camp on a 'Johnny Pye' bus from Heswall*[PSN]

Right:
In September 1923 details of the scheme for building the Edgeworth Estate were announced by Lord Leverhulme. Building commenced in 1924, and the first house Dunfield *was ready for occupation on 6 December*[PSN]

Left: *A dredger* Sand Swallow *came into operation to clear silt from Bromborough Pool. The mast, funnel and crane jib were all fashioned to lower, so that at high water she could pass freely beneath the old Bromborough Pool Bridge, which carried the New Chester Road over the inlet*[PSN]

Below: *Seen here, accompanied by members of the official party, the Hon W Hulme Lever formally hands over* Dunfield *to its new occupants Mr and Mrs Dunbar and their daughter*[PSN]

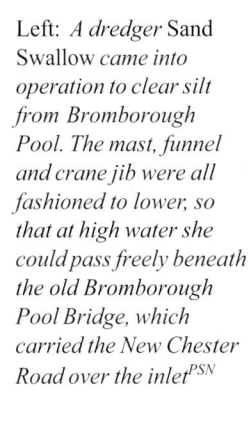

Feb 17	Meeting of the Thurstaston Camp Committee decided there should be 5 Special Weekends - Easter, Whit Week, August Bank Holiday, Closing Weekend and the Gala. No bookings to be taken earlier than four days before each
Mar 19	Lord Leverhulme welcomed back to Port Sunlight after his 6 month tour of West Africa
Mar 26	Fire at No.2 Oil Mill in the Port Sunlight factory
May	British Oil & Cake Mills Ltd taken over by Lever Brothers
May 7	**Death of Viscount Leverhulme in London**
May 11	Lord Leverhulme laid to rest in a tomb at Christ Church, next to his wife Lady Lever (*see poster & photos*)
May 17	Memorial Service to the late Lord Leverhulme held in Christ Church
Jul 1	Formation of Port Sunlight Management Board
Jul 19	The Port Sunlight Company of the 4/5th Cheshires started their 5th post-war camp at the Forydd, Rhyl
Dec	Over 230,000 people had visited Lady Lever Art Gallery during the year

—	Work started early in the year on the new Bromborough Dock scheme
—	Greendale Road was widened and the poplar trees which lined both sides of the road were removed (*see photo opposite*)
—	Houses built: 3-6 Greendale Road; 47-57 Primrose Hill and 10-14 Queen Mary's Drive

Above: *A Liverpool lady was the lucky 100,000th Visitor for 1925 to Port Sunlight for which she received a casket of Port Sunlight products* (see inset top left of picture)PSN

On the 7 May Lord Leverhulme, founder of Lever Brothers and Port Sunlight, died at his home in London at the age of 74. He was buried alongside his wife in the Narthex at Christ Church, Port Sunlight. Thousands of mourners filed passed his coffin which lay in state at the Lady Lever Art Gallery prior to the funeral

Above: *Lord Leverhulme's coffin leaving the Lady Lever Gallery after lying in state*

Above: *Lord Leverhulme's funeral cortege passing through Port Sunlight Village*

Right & Below: *Lord Leverhulme's coffin being borne into Christ Church by Levers' Barge Captains*

FUNERAL

OF THE

LATE VISCOUNT LEVERHULME

The Funeral of the LATE VISCOUNT LEVERHULME
Will take place on

MONDAY, the 11th instant,

At Christ Church, Port Sunlight
AT 1-45 P.M.

The Works and Offices will be closed the whole of the day on Monday, the 11th.

OWING to the large number of relatives and friends of the Family, representatives of Lever Brothers Limited and Associated Companies, and Official Deputations who will attend the ceremony, and owing to the limited accommodation of the Church, the Directors deeply regret that it will only be possible to provide space inside the Church for the oldest employees of the Company, to whom cards of admission will be sent, but so far as space is available accommodation will be provided in the Churchyard and the immediate vicinity of the Church for all others.

It has been arranged that the Body will lie in the Central Hall of the Lady Lever Art Gallery on Sunday, the 10th, between the hours of 10 a.m. and 5 p.m., when the Gallery will be open to the Public to pass by the Coffin, and thus afford an opportunity for all to pay tribute to the memory of our beloved chairman. It is suggested that wreaths be sent to the Lady Lever Art Gallery.

On Monday, the funeral cortege will enter the Village by way of the Wiend, and will proceed along Greendale Road and the Causeway, past the War Memorial to Christ Church.

LEVER BROTHERS LIMITED

Feb 15		Following an abnormally high tide, the barge *Omo* went aground on the bank of Wharf Island in Bromborough Pool – with the help of the dredger *Sand Swallow* she was rescued at the next high tide
Feb 25		Serious fire at No.1 Oil Mill where both Port Sunlight Fire Engines were on the spot 3 minutes after the alarm was raised and worked continuously for 34 hours helped by a Birkenhead Brigade motor pump and crew – fire started in one of the upper storeys and spread to the next floor up and down. The fire crews managing to confine the fire to these 3 floors
Apr		Lever Brothers' Sewing room started
Apr		At the Works Employees' Advisory Committee it was confirmed that employees could only smoke in the areas where notices were placed to that effect - smoking elsewhere was not allowed
Apr		Memorial windows in the apse of St George's Congregational Church in Thornton Hough unveiled in memory of the late Lord Leverhulme
May		Factory operated through the General Strike helped by owners of private cars volunteering to carry hundreds of workers to and from work (*see photo next page*)
May 30		A group of 250 members of the Halifax Building Society visited the village (*see photo next page*)
May 21		Over 900 children at the the New Chester Road Schools celebrated Empire Day (*see photo next page*)
Jun 23		The Works and Office Advisory Committee visited Lever Brothers' Gwernymynyd Quarries in North Wales (*see photo*)
Jul 12		The Works Employees Advisory Committee proposed that they treat 1,000 children from the Charles Thompson Mission in Birkenhead to a day out at Thurstaston Camp
Jul 29		The people of Port Sunlight Village and Bromborough Port Estate voted to elect the Village Advisory Committee
Sep 4		First joint Fire Brigade demonstration by brigades from Liverpool, Birkenhead, Wallasey, Port Sunlight, Bootle, Hoylake and Chester held at the the Recreation Ground with proceeds in aid of the Birkenhead hospitals (*see photo*)
Sep 18		First Founder's Day (on the Saturday nearest to his birthday) held at the Recreation Ground
Oct 2		The 1,700 delegates to the No.IV District of the St John's Ambulance Brigade's Conference in the Auditorium was the largest group of visitors for 3 years (*see photo next page*)
—		Patients at the Port Sunlight Cottage Hospital were supplied with headphones by the Hospital Collection Committee to listen to the wireless
—		The 39th Wirral Agricultural Society's Show was held at the Recreation Grounds with rain falling throughout the day
—		The winner of the Port Sunlight Girl Guides' balloon race had the postcard attached to their balloon returned from Droitwich
—		Houses built: 6a-6h Greendale Road; 15-22 Queen Mary's Drive 1-5 & 2-4 Windy Bank rebuilt

Above: From the stand at the Oval the crowds watch a demonstration given by five brigades from Liverpool, Birkenhead, Wallasey, Port Sunlight, Bootle, Hoylake and Chester. Proceeds from this first joint fire brigades demonstration were in aid of the Birkenhead hospitals. Among the spectators were Lord and Lady Leverhulme, the Mayor and Mayoress of Birkenhead and the Mayors of Wallasey and Bootle

Above: This photograph shows members of the Works and Office Advisory Committee at Port Sunlight, visiting the Quarries at Gwernymynyd, near Mold, North Wales. Lever Brothers had bought the quarries in 1916 where silica rock was excavated. It was then transported to Port Sunlight and used in the production of Monkey Brand and Vim, giving them an abrasive quality 'which made pots and pans shine like polished silver'. After the visit the party retired to the Loggerheads Inn for lunch[PSN]

Above: As a result of the decision to widen Greendale Road in early 1925, the workmen are seen here removing the poplar trees. The Post Office can be seen on the right[PSN]

Above: Members of the Halifax Permanent Building Society are seen on 30 June 1930 descending the steps from Port Sunlight Station where they arrived on a special train in the afternoon. After touring the works, they had tea in Hulme Hall then proceeded to a conference of Building Societies at Southport. PSN

Above: Another picture of the guides who conducted visitors on tours of Port Sunlight works. They were kept busy with over 110,000 visitors for the year of 1926 with the 100,000th visitor being presented with a large casket of Lever products. PSN

Above: Port Sunlight received large numbers of visitors, from individuals to large groups who were conducted on a tour of Port Sunlight Village and the works. One of the largest groups of visitors was the 1,700 delegates to a conference of No.IV District of the St John's Ambulance Brigade on 2 October 1926. The delegates toured the village and works in the morning and can be seen at the conference after lunch which was held in the Auditorium. PSN

Above: Over 900 children attended the Empire Day celebrations at the New Chester Road Schools on 21 May. The entertainment started with an Empire Day song followed by the crowning of the May Queen, maypole dancing and an Empire pageant. The celebration concluded with old English songs. At Church Drive Schools there was also an Empire pageant but on a smaller scale with Britannia pictured above and representatives dressed in costumes from various nations of the Empire, as well as the Boys' Brigade, Scouts and Girl Guides PSN

Above: Due to the General Strike, when the normal public transport services were not available, owners of private motor cars, motor cycles and other vehicles came to the rescue by conveying people to work. These girls seem to be enjoying themselves despite their somewhat primitive mode of transport – the only other way to travel was on foot. PSN

1927

Feb 21 At the Village Advisory Committee, in response to a request for a putting green in the village, it was pointed out that there was already a putting green at the Recreation Grounds, but was little used

Mar 9 The Port Sunlight News' 'Ladies Page' advised that the new shades for stockings were Muscat (dark fawn), Kasha (fawny grey) and French Nude (pinkish grey) - some fashion tips included ''high-crowned hats are still much worn, but a compromise is being effected by crushing or denting the top of the crown" and ''the smartest women are having handbags made of the same material as their coats or frocks"

Mar 23 It was announced that the Cottage Hospital was to be known as The Hospital, Port Sunlight

Mar 23 The Port Sunlight News advertised for sale: 2 The Wiend Bebington - Modern house: 2 entertaining rooms, 4 bedrooms, bathroom etc, pantry, kitchenette & outside washhouse, back garden well stocked with fruit trees - room for garage. Price £900

May 9 Port Sunlight Railway Station opened to the public with services to Chester and Birkenhead

May 22 Bronze effigy of 1st Lord Leverhulme unveiled at Christ Church by his son, the 2nd Lord Leverhulme

Jun A record 9,000 visitors were received at Port Sunlight in one week mainly due to the celebrations for Birkenhead's Jubilee Week

Jul 16 Over 1,000 children from Charles Thompson's Mission enjoyed a day at Thurstaston Camp

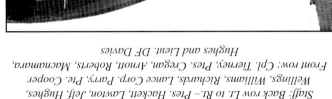

Above: Port Sunlight Boys Brigade winners of the 1927 Bugle-Major's Staff: Back row Lt. to Rt— Ptes. Hackett, Lawton, Jeff, Hughes, Wellings, Williams, Richards, Lance Corp. Parry, Pte. Cooper
Front row: Cpl. Tierney, Ptes. Cregan, Arnott, Roberts, Macnamara, Hughes and Lieut. DF Davies

Above: This is the damage caused to the sheds at the Recreation Grounds following a terrific gale on 28 October 1927 PSN

1927

Aug During Bank Holiday weekend the 2nd Lord Leverhulme opened a newly equipped 'convalescent hut' at the Thurstaston Camp

Sep 17 Over 25,000 people assembled at the Port Sunlight Recreation Ground for 'Founder's Day' celebrations which included a motor-cycle carnival and gymnastic display, with Ryan's Fancy Fair at the southerly end

Sep 22 Lord Leverhulme and party sailed from Southampton to Cape Town aboard the Arundel Castle for the first part of their Africa Tour

Sep 28 Advertised 'For Sale' in the Port Sunlight News: House near Raby Mere (2 miles Port Sunlight). Three bedrooms, two entertaining, bath, conservatory, large garden, fruit trees. £790.

Oct 26 Another house advertised through the Port Sunlight News - Semi-Detached Villa. Freehold: containing one sitting room, dining room, kitchen, three bedrooms, bathroom (tiled) outside washhouse with gas boiler, small garage, electric light fittings. Beautiful gardens back and front with wireless pole sunk in concrete. £730 - 4 Stonehill Avenue East, Lower Bebington

Above: The Port Sunlight News describes the girls working on the Vinolia Company Easter promotion UNI: ''The bevy of girls shown in the photograph are engaged in packing eggs cunningly designed in toilet soap, each egg being placed in a pretty oval glass cup, and with the egg and cup, is wrapped a couple of little yellow life-like chicks PSN

Above: The Port Sunlight Fire and Ambulance Brigade is pictured in 1927 when the brigade consisted of:- 3 officers, 14 firemen and 16 auxiliary firemen and watchmen – all qualified St John Ambulance men; 2 motor fire engines and 1 motor ambulance

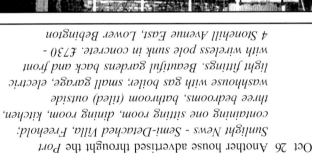

Jan 25 The Estate Department took over the care and
       maintenance of the Churchyard, with the expenses
       being borne by Lever Brothers
Mar 29 King Amanullah and Queen Surayya of Afghanistan
       visited the factory
May 12 New Bowling Green opened in Bolton Road
Jul   A set of six postcard views of Port Sunlight priced
       2d each published by Judges (*see photos*)
Jul 12 Royal visit from King Ofori Atta from the Gold Coast
       with his chief bodyguard Jasehene Kwadjo Pippim
       (*see photo*)
Sep 3 First UK manufacture of *Lux Toilet Soap* (*see advert
       opposite*)
Nov 18 The Birkenhead Boys' Brigade Battalion Church
       Parade at Oxton Road Congregational Church was
       attended by 70 members of the Port Sunlight
       Company
Dec   Record number of visitors to Port Sunlight of
       139,000 during 1928

The Post Office, Port Sunlight

Set of six postcard views of Port Sunlight published by Judges
priced 2d each. Although published in 1928, the pictures of
Greendale Road were clearly taken some time previously and
still show the avenue of trees taken down in 1925

Lever Brothers General Offices

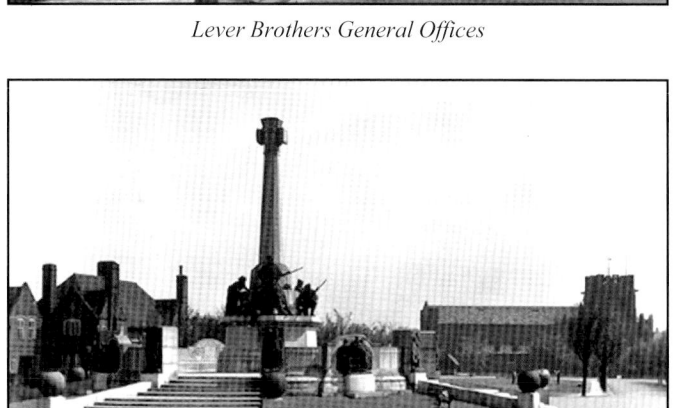

War Memorial and Christ Church, Port Sunlight

The Dell, Port Sunlight

War Memorial, Port Sunlight

Lady Lever Art Gallery, Port Sunlight

Above: *Lord Leverhulme's and Lady Lever's Tombs in the Narthex at Christ Church Port Sunlight (the railings seen today were added more recently to protect the bronze effegies)*

Above: *King Nana Ofori Atta, the monarch from the Gold Coast is seen wearing a gold studded crown under the Royal Umbrella at the Wharf. With the King on his visit to Port Sunlight on 12 July 1928 was his bodyguard Jasehene Kwadjo Pippim and others from this African country[PSN]*

Above: *This is an interior view of the Mac Fisheries' shop in the former Employees' Provident Store on the corner of Bridge Street and Bolton Road. The* Port Sunlight News *of the time describes this store as follows:*
"The shop opens its arms to you; it has a white-clothed staff, eager to welcome you and render service. Cleanliness everywhere. If you have not been, just go and look at our new stores. It is a real visit of pleasure and, I venture to think, cannot be beaten on this or the other side of the river as a modern village store. Mac Fisheries in Bolton Road is a revelation in progress".[PSN]

The First UK manufacture of Lux Toilet Soap[UNI] *was on 3 September 1928 and 'The Story of Lux Toilet Soap' is reproduced from a 'Souvenir of Port Sunlight'*

THE STORY OF LUX TOILET SOAP

LUX Toilet Soap has created as striking a revolution in its class as Sunlight Soap created among household soaps forty years ago. In the United States of America, in Canada, Australia and South Africa, in India and China and Persia equally with the United Kingdom and the countries of Europe it has been enthusiastically acclaimed. Women, the world over, are wondering how such luxuriousness of lather, delicacy of perfume and beauty of appearance and packing can be combined at so low a price.

Its snow-white colour testifies to its purity, and doubtless is more convincing to its millions of users than a description of what it is made of and how it is made. But it is the scrupulous care taken in its manufacture that makes Lux Toilet Soap the exquisite soap it is. Its purity has its source in the finest ingredients and a stringent supervision by skilled chemists at every stage of manufacture. First, the ingredients are boiled exactly the length of time necessary for their perfect blending. Then the soap is cooled in frames and cut into long bars. After hardening, these bars are cut into fine strips, which are conditioned—or matured—in a carefully regulated stove. Thence the strips go to the perfumer's room—a highly important stage in the manufacture of Lux Toilet Soap, for it was only after prolonged experiment that its rarely delicate perfume was produced and adopted, and that perfume has done as much to make Lux Toilet Soap famous as its other qualities. The perfume is mixed into the soap, and the strips are worked into a plastic condition between marble mills, emerging as long, beautifully-perfumed white ribbons. The ribbons of soap go into a plodder, and are compressed into solid bars. These are automatically cut into tablet-length pieces, which are picked up by a machine and fed to a stamper. Here the tablets are given their dainty shape and are ready to be enclosed in the famous sampler wrappers and packed ready for dispatch to the shops.

We have followed the course of manufacture of Lux Toilet Soap as a specific illustration of the methods employed in making a toilet soap. There are several other well-known toilet soaps produced in the factory, and they are all subject to that rigorous scientific insistence on quality which governs every manufacturing operation at Port Sunlight.

1929

- Vinolia operation moved from the building on Quarry Road to No.4 Soapery
- The Trustees of the Lady Lever Art Gallery purchased the painting by William Hogarth (1697-1764) entitled "David Garrick in the Green Room of Drury Lane"
- Wood Street was adjudged 'the best row of gardens in the village'

Above: Lever Brothers' Limited new ambulance is pictured outside the Lady Lever Art Gallery upon delivery in October. This new ambulance replaced the one bought in 1921 PSN

Above & Below: Two views of the airey open-air wards at the Port Sunlight Village Hospital which, in 1929 had been open for over 21 years

1929

Jan 23   The Ladies' Page of the *Port Sunlight News* offered hints on "Etiquette For The Sick Room" - *'Never walk about on tip-toe; see that your shoes are not of the squeaky kind and just walk as lightly and naturally as possible. Also Don't conduct a conversation with a third party in whispers - the patient would rather hear a low, well-modulated voice than a sibilant hiss'*

Jan 27   The Port Sunlight Boys' Brigade paraded at Bebington Station - then with the Bebington Church Lads' Brigade marched to the Claughton Music Hall near Charing Cross, Birkenhead for a meeting of 1,000 boys from various associations and later returned again on foot to Port Sunlight through the pouring rain!

Feb/Mar   After an extended frost, Lord Leverhulme opened the lake at *Thornton Manor* to paying skaters which resulted in a £250 donation to Neston Cottage Hospital

Feb 19   The Port Sunlight Golf Association decided that lady employees and others connected with the business were eligible for election as associates

Mar 20   An article in *Port Sunlight News* called for a meeting to establish a Port Sunlight Golf Club

May   The Crosville Motor Company added a special bus service between New Ferry and Heswall and Thornton Hough which was appreciated by employees living in those areas

May 1   Mr James Darcy Lever died - he was the eldest son of the late James Darcy Lever and nephew of the 1st Lord Leverhulme

May 11   Planters Sports Club's new Pavilion opened

Jun 5   A holiday hint for ladies in the *Port Sunlight News* advised *"never put summer frocks into an already bulging suit-case. Put them in an envelope and post them"*

Jul 15   Mr Sandy Herd, who won the Open Golf Championship in 1902, visited Port Sunlight to give his advice on the laying-out of a 9-hole course on the Edgeworth Estate

Aug   Some 12,000 scouts from the World Jamboree at Arrowe Park visited the factory. During the Jamboree Lever Brothers allowed Thurstaston Camp to be used by 1,600 campers from the Holborn Scouts and West Riding of Yorkshire Scouts

Aug   *Spital Hall* was placed at the disposal of Miss Royden of *Frankby Hall* who ran it as an hospital in connection with the Jamboree

Aug   Electricity replaced gas in Port Sunlight Village (*see photo opposite*)

Aug 30   Lord Leverhulme opened the new premises of the United Comrades' Federation in Hesketh Hall

Sep   A record number of 4,519 campers and over 6,000 visitors attended Thurstaston during the 1929 season

Sep 2   Formal agreement with the Dutch Margarine Union to form Margarine Union Ltd, forerunner of Unilever

Oct   New ambulance for Lever Brothers delivered (*see photo*)

Dec   It was announced that a record number of 153,300 visitors had passed through the works in 1929

Above: *Another milestone in Port Sunlight's history was reached when the village changed its power from gas to electricity. Although electicity had been installed at the factory since 1889, the village had relied on gas to light and power the houses and buildings. A crowd has gathered in the background to view the proceedings[PSN]*

Right: *Some of the girls from Planters are showing off their 'up-todate' working clothes[PSN]*

Below: *A group of Scouts from India are seen posing on the steps of the Lady Lever Art Gallery during their tour of the village and works. Over 9,000 scouts attending the Arrowe Park International Scout Jamboree visited Port Sunlight during the week. Mr GB Lissenden, Lever Brothers' Traffic Manager, acted as chairman of the Transport Committee for the Jamboree[PSN]*

Jan 12 Rev Thomas Webster commenced his Ministry at Christ Church Port Sunlight *(see photo)*

Jan 28 At the Advisory Committee reference was made again to the serious consequences of smoking in the factory and employees' co-operation was asked in eliminating the practice

Mar The Joint Railway Companies increased rail fares - Port Sunlight to Birkenhead Town from 3d to 3.5d

Mar 5 The Margarine Union Ltd formally changed its name to Unilever Limited

Apr 2 George Duckworth, the famous England and Lancashire wicket-keeper, gave the Port Sunlight Recreation members a lantern lecture in the Lyceum on the recent test match series in Australia

Apr 5 For the first time Thurstaston Camp opened before Easter weekend (by 2 weeks)

May 24 The Port Sunlight Radio Club visited the White Star Liner *Cedric* at Liverpool Landing Stage

Jun 5 *Thornton Manor* Gardens open to the public at a charge of 6d entrance - proceeds to local charities

Jun 22 A 'Moth' type aeroplane returning to Hooton experienced engine trouble and crash-landed in a field on the east side of the railway siding near Port Causeway. Pilot and passenger escaped injury

Jun 30 Atta of the Igbirra tribe of Nigeria and his wife, Mamuna, visited Port Sunlight

Jul The drawing '*Preaching to the Roundheads*' by John Everett Millais and '*The Three Green Domes*' by W Russel Flint RA were added to the Lady Lever Collection by the 2nd Viscount Leverhulme

Jul 29 Swimming competition between Cheshire and Lancashire held at Port Sunlight Baths

Aug The Port Sunlight Golf Course opened on part of the Edgeworth Estate *(see photo)*

Sep Membership for the new golf club closed as there were 250 members

Sep 13 The Lord Leverhulme Memorial was unveiled on Founder's Day outside the Lady Lever Art Gallery *(see photo opposite)*

Sep 22 First water let into the new Bromborough Dock

Oct 13 The easterly half of the new bridge over Bromborough Pool was opened to traffic *(see photo opposite)*

Nov 1 The initial effort to raise funds for the first training of Guide Dogs for the Blind was by the Alsatian League of Great Britain who gave them all its profit from a show held in the Auditorium Port Sunlight *(see poster)*

Nov 16 The Port Sunlight Boys' Brigade, Girl Guides and Brownies witnessed the dedication of the Girl Guides' new District Flag at Christ Church Port Sunlight

Dec It was estimated that 140,000 visitors from all parts of the world were received at Port Sunlight during 1930

— Saddle tank locomotive *Wynnstay* purchased 2nd hand from Wynnstay Collieries in Denbighshire

Right: *Port Sunlight Oils & Cake Mills in 1930*

Above: *This poster advertises an Alsation Dog Show which was the first ever fund-raising event in this country for the Guide Dogs for the Blind which was held at the Auditorium, Port Sunlight on Saturday 1 November*

Above: *A lady golfer on the Port Sunlight Golf Club course which opened on part of the Edgeworth Estate in August 1930[PSN]*

Left: *Seen here the easterly half of the 'White Bridge' on New Chester Road after opening in October 1930. Built by Cheshire County Council at a cost of £50,000, it was deliberately built tall enough for vessels with high masts & funnels to pass under[PSN]*

Left: *The Rev Thomas Webster commenced his ministry at Christ Church in January 1930*

Above: *The New Chester Road Bridge can be seen under construction on the right, with Prices' Works at Bromborough Pool in the distance[PSN]*

"I WANT A TABLET OF SOAP, PLEASE!"
"WILL YOU HAVE IT SCENTED?"
"NO, I'LL TAKE IT WITH ME!"

Above: *A soap comic postcard posted in 1930*

Seen here being unveiled on 13 September 1930, this memorial to the first Lord Leverhulme stands outside the western entrance to the Lady Lever Gallery. It was designed by James Lomax Simpson, Lord Leverhulme's godson and the company architect, and sculptured by Sir William Read Dick. The tall polished black granite column supports a figure representing 'Inspiration' whilst the figures at the base, covered by a Union Jack, represent 'Industry, Education, Charity and Art'

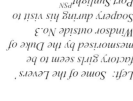

*Left: Some of the Levers' factory girls seen to be mesmorised by the Duke of Windsor outside No.3 Soapery during his visit to Port Sunlight*PSN

Above: The Prince of Wales presents a New Standard to the British Legion watched by members of the United Comrades Federation with Lord Leverhulme looking on

Below: The Port Sunlight Firemen are sitting on Lever Brothers' two Fire Engines outside the District Bank in Greendale Road. The Levers' logo can be seen below the driver of the front vehicle

Left: This postcard view of the Lady Lever Art Gallery, which was posted in 1931, was taken from a railway train. The picture had been taken after the Windy Bank houses had been moved to improve the view of the gallery, but before the Leverhulme Memorial was built in 1930 (compare with picture opposite)

*Right: Lever Brothers' workers and villagers pose for the photographer in Greendale Road. The District Bank, later the Nat West, is on the left*PSN

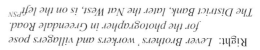

Jan 16	First vessel unloaded at the new Bromborough Dock
Apr 2	1931 Thurstaston Holiday Camp season starts - cost for single person one shilling per night; cost for families on early application; beds & bedding provided; campers to cook their own food
Apr 17	Bromborough Dock officially opened. Railway passenger carriage was converted for use as a First-aid Station at Bromborough Dock
Jun 11	Prince George (later the Duke of Kent) visited works
Jul	Superannuation Fund introduced for managers and staff
Nov 4	Prince of Wales (later Duke of Windsor) visited works (*see photo*)
Dec	During 1931 there were a total of 1112 births which included two sets of twins at Bromborough Pool Maternity Home

—	Memorial Window in memory of the 1st Lord Leverhulme installed in the South Transept of Christ Church
—	Gladstone Hall extended southwards and the original platform replaced by a new stage – new toilets built on the site of the original pantry and the Green Room built behind the stage

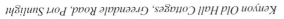

Whitfield & Cannon, wholesale stationers and photographers of Wallasey, produced a series of 14 postcard views of Port Sunlight in 1931. This gives a good idea of how the village looked then

The War Memorial, Port Sunlight

Kenyon Old Hall Cottages, Greendale Road, Port Sunlight

The Lady Lever Art Gallery, Port Sunlight

The Post Office, Port Sunlight

The Leverhulme Memorial and Art Gallery, Port Sunlight

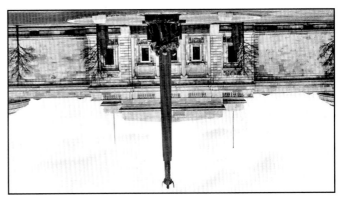

Main Entrance General Offices, Port Sunlight

Christ Church, Port Sunlight

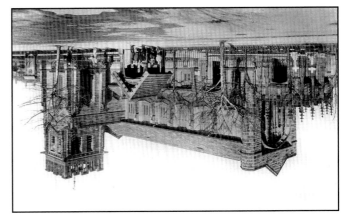

Park Road, Port Sunlight

1931

1931

Above: The 'Silver Wedding' Fountain is pictured in front of Port Sunlight Railway Station having been moved here from the top of the Dell. It was moved again in 1932 to its present position in front of the bowling green facing Greendale Road

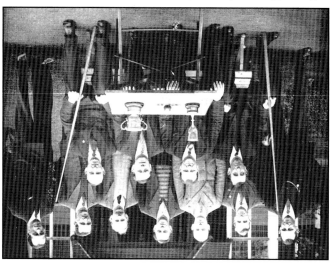

Above: The United Comrades' Federation 'A' Billiards team which won the League and Charity Competition are as follows:
Standing: FC Underwood, E Lewis (Chairman), JL Podmore, GA Cox, JH Maybury, T Christian, HA Brandon
Seated: J Ackroyd, J King, G Brown (Captain), W Christian

Above: The designers for the United Comrades' Federation new bowling green shelter decided to resort to the old-fashioned type of thatched roof, seen here in the spring of 1932

Above: The Birkenhead Corporation buses, Nos. 52 and 54 Leyland Lion LT2s single-decker buses, are seen on the right waiting outside Port Sunlight Station. These rear-entrance buses came into service in June 1930 and seated 35 passengers

Jan	The death was announced of Corporal Frederick G Room VC, in Bristol. During the First World War he was a patient in Hulme Hall which had been converted into a Military Hospital
Jan 4	The Sick Club and Doctor's Surgery at 1 Boundary Road closed and was moved to the Port Sunlight Hospital
Jan 29	Lady Lever Art Gallery re-opened having had the interior decorated, the picture glasses cleaned and frames touched up
Feb	The Liverpool and District Aero Club advertised in *Port Sunlight News* for parties of 10 to 20 to be entertained at Hooton Aerodrome at 7/6d (37.5p) per head. This included an aerial joy-ride (not the one minute flip) followed by tea in the clubhouse
Mar 5	Port Sunlight AF Team won the Cheshire Amateur Cup beating Thorndale 3-2 at Tranmere Rovers' ground
Apr	Bromborough Dock handled over 60,000 tons of traffic since the beginning of the year
Apr 27	Semi-detached House at 8 The Wiend, Lr Bebington advertised for sale in the *Port Sunlight News* with 2 reception rooms, large hall, 4 bedrooms, kitchen, scullery, bathroom etc. Gas, electric light with garden back and front - price £825
May	The shelters for the United Comrades Federation new Bowling Green built, complete with thatched roof *(see photo)*
May 25	An advert in the *Port Sunlight News* offered a *Charming Detached Villa - 'Woburn' Brookhurst Road Bromborough - 2 reception rooms, four bedrooms, garage, electric light, telephone, half an acre of well stocked garden with tennis lawn and swimming pool all for £1,400*
May 28	March-past at the Recreation Ground for the 1st and 2nd Port Sunlight Girl Guide Company to celebrate the 21st anniversary of the founding of the Girl Guide Movement *(see photo opposite)*
May 29	Port Sunlight Brownies and Girl Guides attended a special service to celebrate the Girl Guide Movement's 21st birthday
Jun 18	Inspection of the Cheshire County Nursing and Ambulance Brigade (No.4 District) at the Recreation Ground
Jun 24	Lever Brothers' Chiropody Clinic started
Aug 9	The Furness Withy boat *Nova Scotia* was the first passenger liner to enter Bromborough Dock
Sep 17	Founder's Day Celebrations at Port Sunlight Recreation Ground was led by the full massed band of HM Coldstream Guards
Oct	The oil painting *The Sampler* by L Campbell Taylor RA was purchased for the Lady Lever Collection by the Trustees
—	The Bandstand at the centre of The Diamond was taken down (the columns were later reused on the original Stork Margerine Offices on Stadium Road Bromborough – see 1953)
—	The 'Silver Wedding Fountain' moved for the second time – to the front of the bowling green *(see photo)*

Above: *Poster advertising United Comrades'
Federation Dinner and Film Show in the
Men's Dining Hall on 8 October 1932*[UNI]

Left:
*This campaign
poster issued by
the Health and
Cleanliness
Council in
1932*[UNI]

Above: *Tom Jones and Bill Edwards are pictured in front of the Lever
Brothers Motor Fire Engine on the occasion of their retirement from
the Port Sunlight Fire Brigade having served the brigade for some
40-odd years between them*[UNI]

Above: *Enjoying a taste of the Guides' 21st Birthday Cake, the
District Commissioner, Miss Jolly, is joined by a group of Brownies at
the Recreation Ground on 28 May 1932*[UNI]

Right:
*This is an artist's
impression of a scheme to
build a large water feature
in the centre of The
Diamond. It was never
completed apart from the
terrace at the southerly end
but is the possible reason
for the bandstand being
demolished in 1932*[UNI]

Feb 16   Two locomotives *No.4* & *No.5* delivered second-
         hand to Port Sunlight. Previously operated by
         William Gossage & Sons of Widnes, which Lever
         had purchased in 1919. The Gossage name was
         removed but, unusually for Port Sunlight, the
         locomotives were never given names

Apr 27   A tablet was unveiled at Christ Church in memory of
         the late John Gray, a former Director of Lever Bros
         and company Vice-Chairman, by his son, George
         Gray

Apr 27   The new Bowling Green and Club House on
         Boundary Road, built for the United Comrades
         Federation, was officially opened by the President
         the 2nd Lord Leverhulme

May 16   The Emir of Katsina visited Port Sunlight with his
         wife, Madaike, 2 of his sons, Nagogo and Lamba,
         his brother Kankiya and his wife, his headman, and
         his two grandsons Ibrahim and Usuman. Katsina
         was an ancient state in the province of Kano under
         the British Protectorate of Northern Nigeria

Jul   1 Five of Lever Brothers' horses were entered in the
         Bebington Show with 4 of them carrying off an
         award

July 22 Start of the Port Sunlight Boys' Brigade 34th
         Annual camp held at Stoke Flemming, South Devon

Aug 17   The 100,000th visitor to the Port Sunlight factory for
         1933 was presented with a special casket

Aug 29   James Rowland, an apprentice in the Engineering
         Department and troop leader with the 60th
         Birkenhead Scouts, was presented with the Silver
         Cross Scout Medal by the Chief Scout, Lord Baden-
         Powell, for saving a 4-year old boy from drowning in
         a pit at New Ferry (*see photo opposite*)

Sep 11   The Girls' Social Club changed its name to the Port
         Sunlight Social Club (for Women and Girls)

Sep 16   On Founder's Day the second Lord Leverhulme
         opened the new extension to the billiard room at the
         Social Club which housed four tables

Oct 9   The Works Advisory Committee reported that due
         to damage in the village done by children and the
         accumulation of litter in Quarry Road and The Dell
         after the lunch hour, the Company felt it necessary
         to have someone in attendance to watch these
         points

Nov   The Trustees added the painting *Cluanie* by Sir
         David Young Cameron to the Lady Lever Collection.
         Completed in 1930, it was considered amongst the
         best by this famous Scottish painter

Dec   It was announced that during 1933 over 148,076
         visitors passed through the works

Dec 12   Serious fire at Bromborough Dock

—   Terraced garden and ornamental arch at end of the
         Diamond opened (*see photo*) [now houses the
         Hillsborough Memorial Garden]

—   Provident Fund introduced to provide pensions for
         employees

Above: *This ornamental archway at the southerly end of
The Diamond was opened in 1933. The War Memorial can
be seen beyond the girls and the Lady Lever Art Gallery in
the far distance*[UNI]

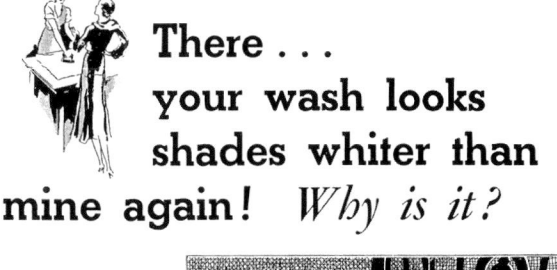
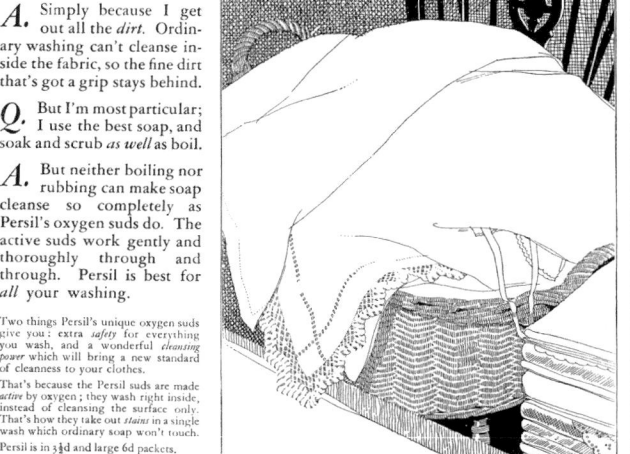
Right: *In 1919, Lever Brothers had acquired Crosfields Chemicals
and with it the patent rights and trade marks for* Persil[UNI] *in the UK.
Originally invented in Germany in 1903, the name was derived
from its two main ingredients PERborate and SILicate*

Above: Port Sunlight Lady Cricketers pose for the camera in 1933 *UNI*

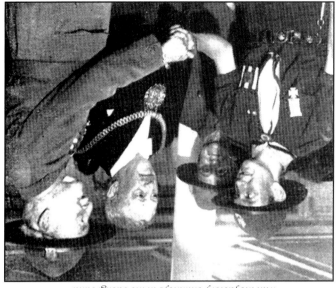

Above: Seen here receiving his award from the Chief Scout, Lord Baden-Powell, James Rowland was also presented with a gold watch by Lord Leverhulme on behalf of the Company in recognition of his gallantry in saving a young boy's life *UNI*

Above: Children's Day outside Christ Church Port Sunlight on 11 June 1933 with the Minister Rev Thomas Webster looking on *UNI*

Above: Sheep grazing in the middle of Port Sunlight Village in 1933 with the factory chimneys in the background *UNI*

Above: An aerial view of Port Sunlight factory taken in the early 1930s with Prices' Works and Bromborough Pool Village in the background *UNI*

The "No-Scum" way with Rinso

The new way to wash-up

Thousands of women who already use Rinso for washing have discovered that the old way of washing-up, too, is has the most wonderful effect . . . The new way of washing-up soon forms a scum of grease on the water, makes dishes smeary and dirty as they are drawn out. But Rinso lather absorbs grease, so that it cannot form a scum on the water – dishes come out absolutely clean and sparkling . . . Rinso is gentle to hands, too . . . Every day thousands more women are doing their washing-up this new NO-SCUM way.

[UNI]

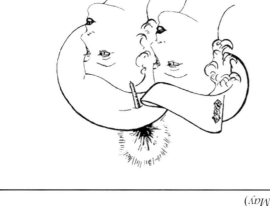

Above: The 'Ladies Page of the Port Sunlight News was a regular feature of the 1930s, always keeping its readers abreast of the latest London fashions. The September 1934 edition shows these designs and gives the following advice: "Just as we are getting used to the flatters of flat shapes, we find that the autumn fashions are going to the other extreme. We shall thus have to adjust our features to elongated headgear [UNI]

Sep 29   Inauguration of rugby at Bromborough Port Sports Club with a match against Old Parkonians

Oct 26   The celebrated film star Anna Neagle and film producer Herbert Wilcox visited Port Sunlight

Oct 30   The first Bibby Bros vessel MV *Staffordshire* to enter Bromborough Dock discharged rice-bran from Burma - the first link between that country and Bromborough Dock

—   Employees' job rates and allowances replace bonus scheme

—   Houses built: 1–18 Duke of York Cottages (see 31 May)

Jan 6   Last night of the Port Sunlight Players Pantomime *Aladdin* during which *Vinolia* Soap Medallions depicting 'Premier Bananas by *Vinolia*' on one side and 'Port Sunlight Players Aladdin' on the other, were distributed among the audience during the singing of 'The Banana Song'

Jan 8   At the Works Employees Advisory Committee it was recommended that a leather attache case filled with the firm's products should replace the present basket given to girls leaving to be married

Jan 24   The old oak tree standing outside Gladstone Hall was taken down due to old age (*see photo opposite*)

Feb 22   The new common room in the Staff Training College was officially opened

Apr 24   Wooden Golf Club Pavilion opened on the Edgeworth course built behind the Vinolia building. It replaced the 2 converted railway coaches used initially (*see photo opposite*)

May 31   Duke of York (later King George VI) visited works and officially opened the Duke of York pensioners' cottages (*see photo opposite*) – he was given 2 dolls, dressed in a miniature reproduction of the Visitors' Guides uniform – one for each of his daughters Princess Elizabeth (the present Queen then aged 8) and Princess Margaret

Jul 5   The new pavilion of the Bromborough Port Sports Club (associated with the Bromborough Margarine Works) was officially opened

Jul 7   The Ladies Page of the *Port Sunlight News* gave a few tips for the ladies when wearing shorts:
1) *The shorts should stop about 2 or 3 inches above the knee* 2) *They should be made of khaki drill, linen, flannel or corduroy velvet* 3) *They should be worn with sports shirt or plain pullover* 4) *They should never be worn with high heels*

Jul 10   Visit to the factory and village of the Emirs of Kano and Gwandu in Nigeria (*see photo opposite*)

Jul 18   King George V accompanied by Queen Mary opened the Mersey Tunnel and on noticing Lord Leverhulme at the Birkenhead entrance his lordship was cordially greeted by both the King and Queen, with the three chatting for several moments. Arrangements were made for Lever employees to view the Royal Train from the high embankment between Bebington and Port Sunlight Stations

Jul 31   The well known band leader, Jack Payne, his wife and band paid a visit to Port Sunlight whilst appearing at the *Empire Theatre, Liverpool*

Aug 18   A hint from the Ladies Page of the Port Sunlight *News – do not make the mistake of enamelling your toe nails when wearing sandals. It makes the feet look much bigger*

Aug 18   An International Motor-Ball Match was played at the Recreation Ground between England and France (played on motor bikes and won by France)

Sep 21   A new *Vinolia Soap* was launched retailing at 6d in a 'dignified blue, buff and gold carton'

Sep 23   The Port Sunlight Fire Brigade was summoned to help deal with the Gresford Colliery Disaster, near Wrexham – management and staff of Lever Bros raised over £330 towards the disaster fund

Above: *On the left of this earlier view of Greendale Road stands an old oak tree in front of Gladstone Hall. There long before the village was built, it eventually succumbed to old age and was taken down in January 1934[UNI]*

Below: *Pictured at the entrance to No.3 Soapery is the Emir of Gwandu on Lord Leverhulme's right, and the Emir of Kano on his left[UNI]*

Above: *An etching showing a 1934 scene in Bromborough Dock[UNI]*

Left: *Outside Gladstone Hall, the Duke of York passes between two lines of Port Sunlight Guides accompanied by Lord Leverhulme on his way to visit the works 31 May 1934[UNI]*

Above: *Rows and rows of clerical workers in the south wing of the Lever Brothers' General offices[UNI]*

Above: *Port Sunlight Pensioners' Club leaving Hulme Hall for an outing to Crossfields on 21 June 1934[UNI]*

Above: *Port Sunlight Bowling Club team pictured in 1934[UNI]*

Feb	It was announced that a Girls' Netball Club had been formed, practising in the gymnasium and playing on the Recreation Grounds where they used the gatehouse as a dressing room
Feb 2	Harold M Abrahams (former British and Olympic Champion) gave an illustrated lecture entitled "World Athletics in 1934"
Feb 19	The Port Sunlight Motor Ambulance answered its 4,000th call since it was first commissioned on 4 August 1920
Mar 19	The SS *Elpenor* discharged her cargo of copra at Bromborough Dock. This took the total tonnage since the dock opened in 1931 to over one million tons
Apr 13	The Port Sunlight Ladies' Hockey Team won the 'Lewis Trophy' beating Cambridge 3-2 in the cup-final at Lewis' ground in Aigburth, Liverpool
Apr 30	Miss ME Donelly, Headmistress of Church Drive School retired after 33 years teaching in the village
May 6	The works closed on the occasion of the King & Queen's Jubilee
May 8	Annual Charity Football match between a Port Sunlight & District XI and Tranmere Rovers was held at the Recreation Ground - Tranmere won 2-0 (*see photo opposite*)
Jun	The launch was announced of a new *Vinolia* quick-lathering shaving stick elegantly wrapped in gold foil, set in a maroon & gold bakelite container and retailing at 9d
Aug 9	The 100,000th visitor to Port Sunlight in 1935 was given a presentation casket
Aug 24	Port Sunlight Ladies' Cricket team, who won the Liverpool Ladies' Cricket League, were presented with the trophy (*see photo opposite*)
Sep 14	Annual Founder's Day celebrations held at the Recreation Grounds
Oct 26	Lady Haig (widow of the late Field-Marshal Earl Haig) visited the Port Sunlight British Legion
—	To commemorate the Silver Jubilee of King George V and Queen Mary, *Vinolia Soap* produced a Soap Jubilee Medal (*see photo*)

Above: *Mr G Stanley Smith, Secretary of the Boys' Brigade organisation and the son of the late Sir William A Smith, founder of the Movement, with Mr DF Davies, Captain of the 1st Port Sunlight Boys' Brigade Company on parade with members of the Company 12 May 1935*[UNI]

Above: *Two of the horses from the Traffic department, "Duke" on the left with his driver Mr Samuel Smith, and "Bob" on the right with driver Mr Herbert Prince. Both gained Special Awards in the Bebington Urban District Garden Fete on Saturday 6 July 1935*[UNI]

Above: *To commemorate the Silver Jubilee of Their Majesties King George and Queen Mary, Soap Jubilee Medals made from a new Vinolia Soap*[UNI] *were produced and distributed to the trade*

Above: *An aerial view of Port Sunlight Village taken in 1935 with the Lady Lever gallery in the foreground and the factory in the distance*

Above: *The Port Sunlight and Tranmere Rovers (seated) teams which took part in the charity match on 8 May in aid of funds for the hospitals. The Tranmere Rovers team included: Gray, Dodd, Spencer, Curtis, Watson, Tyson, Baker, MacDonald, Woodward, Urmson, Eden, and Cooper. Port Sunlight & District XI: T Peevor, R Sumner, WH Lavender, WJ Chetta, J Taylor, K Peters, J Donnelly, J Storey, WE Cooper, HS Bevan, JH Keedwell*[PSN]

Above: *Members of the Port Sunlight and RAF Sealand water polo teams at the Swimming Gala held at Port Sunlight baths on 25 June 1935 (Port Sunlight won 5-2)*[UNI]

Above: *Port Sunlight Ladies' Hockey Team who were winners of the 1st Division of the Liverpool League and the Sir Burton Ellis Cup, and runners-up in the Lewis Cup*

Front row Lt. to Rt.– J Tierney, DH Jones, D Roberts & V Thomas
Centre: H Storey, A Paull, I McManus,(Captain), M Kendall & M Bird
Back: E Dillon, P Shaw, E Reynolds & V Buff[PSN]

Above: *The Port Sunlight Ladies Cricket Team which won the Liverpool Ladies Cricket League in 1933:*
Lt. to Rt. Back row:- Misses L Eastman, L Wotton,and M Morris, Mrs E Browne, Mr F Taylor (umpire) and Miss C Snedker Seated: Misses M Jones & L Youds, Mrs A Moores (President, Liverpool Ladies Cricket League), Misses H Thornton (Captain) & E Hopley. On ground; Miss B Ollerhead & Miss D Jones[PSN]

Below: A view taken in 1936 from the roof of the General Office looking across Port Sunlight towards New Ferry

1936

Jan 1 Lever Brothers introduce a five-day week and reduced hours

Jan 28 **King George V died**

Jan 28 A Memorial Service to King George V was held in Christ Church using the service broadcast from St George's Windsor

Mar The new ship RMS *Queen Mary* is depicted on a special novel *Vinolia* soap 'medal' to honour *Vinolia* as suppliers of their new soap to the new ship (*see photo opposite*)

Apr Port Sunlight Cycling Club formed with a first outing to Farndon

Jul Lady Lever Art Gallery received a donation of Waterford Glass from the late Mr Walter Harding of Nocturoum

Jul 1 The Hon Philip Lever's 21st birthday (*see photo opposite*) – to celebrate, 6,000 Port Sunlight employees and 1,200 children were invited in July to *Thornton Manor* over 4 evenings and 2 afternoons

Jul 2 The Southern Whaling Company's floating factory ship *Southern Empress* discharged whale and sperm oil at Bromborough Dock

Aug Seven members of the Port Sunlight Athletic Club visited Berlin to see the Olympic games

Aug 20 Visit to Port Sunlight Village of 16 members of the Hitler Youth Movement who were offered a welcome return to them or their friends in the future

Aug 21 The GPO installed a 10-position switchboard which then served 700 active lines inside the office and factory, 26 lines to the Rock Ferry Exchange and 16 private lines linked to Unilever House in London and associated companies on Merseyside (*see photo*)

Oct Viscount Leverhulme presented a silver trophy for the inaugural Unilever Drama Festival

Oct The old bridge carrying Bromborough Road over the railway from Storeton Quarries to Bromborough Dock was demolished (*see photo opposite*)

Oct 6 A party of representatives of the German soap and allied industries paid a visit to Port Sunlight

Dec 11 King Edward VIII abdicated

Above: Taken from an advertisement for Vinolia[UNI] products, this shows their range of products for 1936

Above: In August 1936 Lever Brothers installed a new telephone exchange[UNI]

Left: These tablets and soap medals were produced to mark the occasion of a contract for supplies of a new Vinolia[UNI] soap for the 'wonder ship' Queen Mary

Above: The Port Sunlight Junior Football team is photographed in 1936. Back row (Lt. to Rt.): Mr JL McCormack, Bailie, Swindley, Emslie, Mr JG Edwards, Boscoe, Ashworth, Barnes & Mr J McClean Front row: Brown, Stanley, Stewart, Sanders & Winterbottom[UNI]

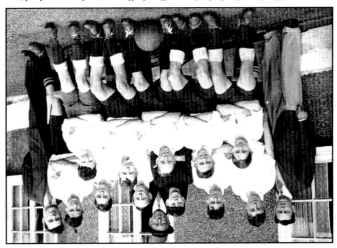

Right: The Hon Philip Lever photographed for his 21st birthday, later to become the third Lord Leverhulme

Above: Bromborough Road Bridge, which originally carried traffic over the Storeton Quarry Tramway, is in the course of demolition in 1936 by workmen employed by Bebington Council. The tramway itself was removed in about 1912 after Sir William Lever bought the railway from the Brocklebank Estate (see 1911)

Right: View of Bromborough Dock taken from an aeroplane in 1937. In the distance can be seen the Port Sunlight village & factory beyond the New Chester Road. Shore Drive and Bolton Road East houses are in the centre, with Prices' works on the left

Above: Marriage of the Hon. Philip Lever to Margaret Ann Moon, he later became the third Lord Leverhulme.

Left: Members of the recently formed Port Sunlight Ladies Lacrosse Club photographed at the Recreation Ground. Miss Pam King, second from right back row, is Captain, and Miss Peggy Jones, third from left in the centre row, is Vice-captain [UNI]

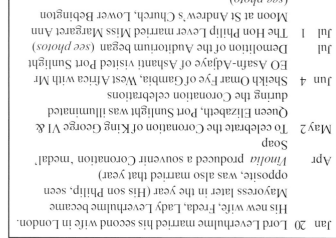

Jan 20   Lord Leverhulme married his second wife in London. His new wife, Freda, Lady Leverhulme became Mayoress later in the year (His son Philip, seen opposite, was also married that year)

Apr   *Vinolia* produced a souvenir Coronation 'medal'

May 2   To celebrate the Coronation of King George VI & Queen Elizabeth, Port Sunlight was illuminated during the Coronation celebrations

Jun 4   Sheikh Omar Fye of Gambia, West Africa with Mr EO Asafu-Adjaye of Ashanti visited Port Sunlight

Jul   Demolition of the Auditorium began (*see photos*)

Jul 1   The Hon Philip Lever married Miss Margaret Ann Moon at St Andrew's Church, Lower Bebington (*see photo*)

Jul 7   Prince Chichibu, brother of the Emperor of Japan paid an unofficial visit to Port Sunlight

Aug 20   A party of German students visited Port Sunlight

Sep 7   Inaugural meeting of the Port Sunlight Ladies' Lacrosse Club

Oct   The second Viscount Leverhulme was installed as Charter Mayor of Bebington (*see photos opposite*)

Oct 28   Dame Sybil Thorndike who was appearing at the Winter Gardens, New Brighton, visited Port Sunlight

Oct 30   Model Aero Club formed in Port Sunlight for boys over 11, the fee being one shilling

—   Port Sunlight Golf Club's wooden clubhouse enlarged (*see photo opposite*)

Right: View of the wooden clubhouse on the Port Sunlight Golf Course with the Lever Brothers' factory in the background

Below: The annual Sunday School Anniversary procession, held on the first Sunday in June, on its way from Christ Church to the War Memorial [UNI]

Above: Freda, Lady Leverhulme, Mayoress

Above: The two pictures above are of the Auditorium, which had provided a venue for Port Sunlight functions for over 30 years, in the process of being demolished. After the site was cleared it was laid out as a sunken garden which is still in use today [UNI]

Above: In October 1937 Lord Leverhulme became the first Mayor of the newly formed Borough of Bebington

Jan	Lever Brothers Port Sunlight Ltd formed
Mar 25	The 2nd Lord Leverhulme, assisted by his son Philip, planted trees by the bowling green on Greendale Road to celebrate his 50th Birthday and also 50 years since the founding of Port Sunlight (*see photo opposite*)
May	Launch of *Sunlight Flakes*
May	Two busts of the original partners of Lever Brothers placed in the Vestibule at Port Sunlight – the late Lord Leverhulme and his brother the late J Darcy Lever
Jun	Jubilee Exhibition at the Lyceum presented Port Sunlight's history (*see photo opposite*)
Jun	*Vinolia Soap* produced a Souvenir Soap for the Empire Exhibition at Glasgow
Jul 4	First Air-raid Precautions when Anti-gas School opened in a portion of the old Bromborough Port Construction Company Offices (*see photo opposite*)
Aug 20	First employees' excursion to the Empire Exhibition at Glasgow
Sep 3	Lever Brothers Cattle Foods, Port Sunlight, exhibited at the centenary Cheshire Agricultural Society's Show at Chester - attended by Lord and Lady Leverhulme (*see photo opposite*)
Sep 3	Second employees' excursion to the Empire Exhibition at Glasgow
Oct	*Port Sunlight News* advertised an almost new house for sale: *"26, Pine Avenue, Bebington with 2 entertaining rooms, kitchen, scullery, etc; 3 bedrooms, separate offices. Wood block floors, panelled hall. Very good garden. Perfect condition £725"*
Oct 3	Hot-pot Supper and Smoking Concert held at Hulme Hall to celebrate Port Sunlight AFC winning the I Zingari League 1st Division Championship
Dec	Work started on demolishing Shakespeare's Cottages to improve the flow of traffic down Wood Street
—	Port Sunlight Players presented *Jack & The Beanstalk* co-written by 'George Hewitt' (Miss Sophie Somers who worked at Levers for over 30 years) and 'William Thornton' (the 2nd Lord Leverhulme) - they wrote at least 6 pantomimes together
—	Houses built: 1-15 Jubilee Crescent erected to celebrate 50 years since the founding of Port Sunlight

Above: *This girl is enjoying herself on a Walls Ice Cream Tricycle (see advert below) at Levers' Thurstaston Camp in the summer of 1938*[UNI]

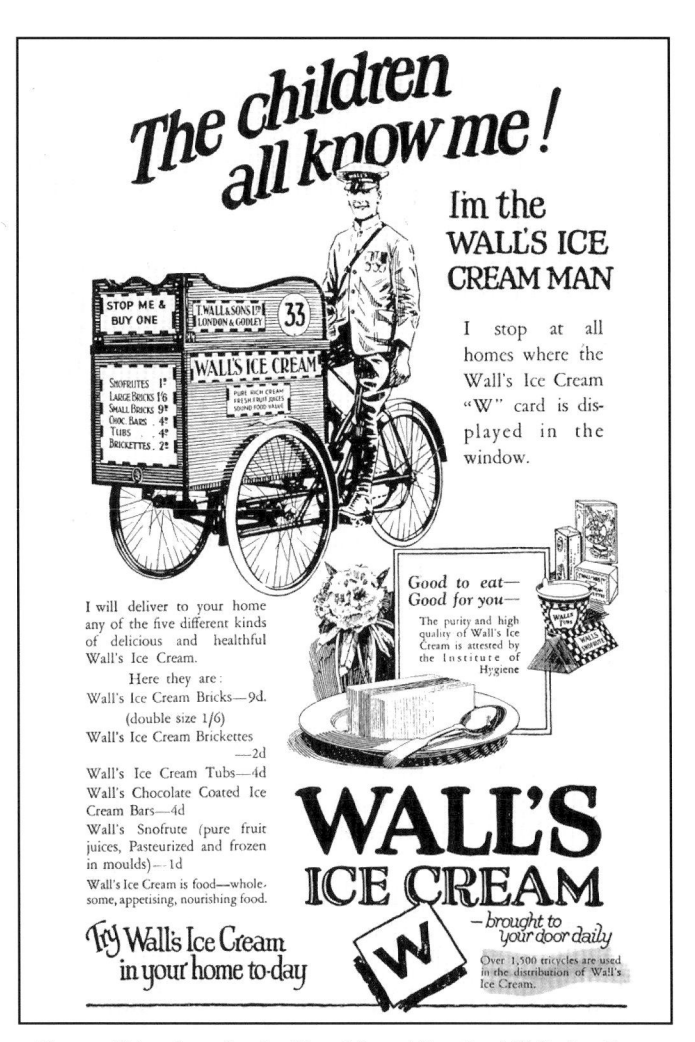

Above: *This advert for the 'Stop Me and Buy One' Walls Ice Cream Man states:* 'I stop at all homes where the Wall's Ice Cream "W" is displayed in the window'. *The local depot was at one time behind the old Vinolia building on Quarry Road*[UNI]

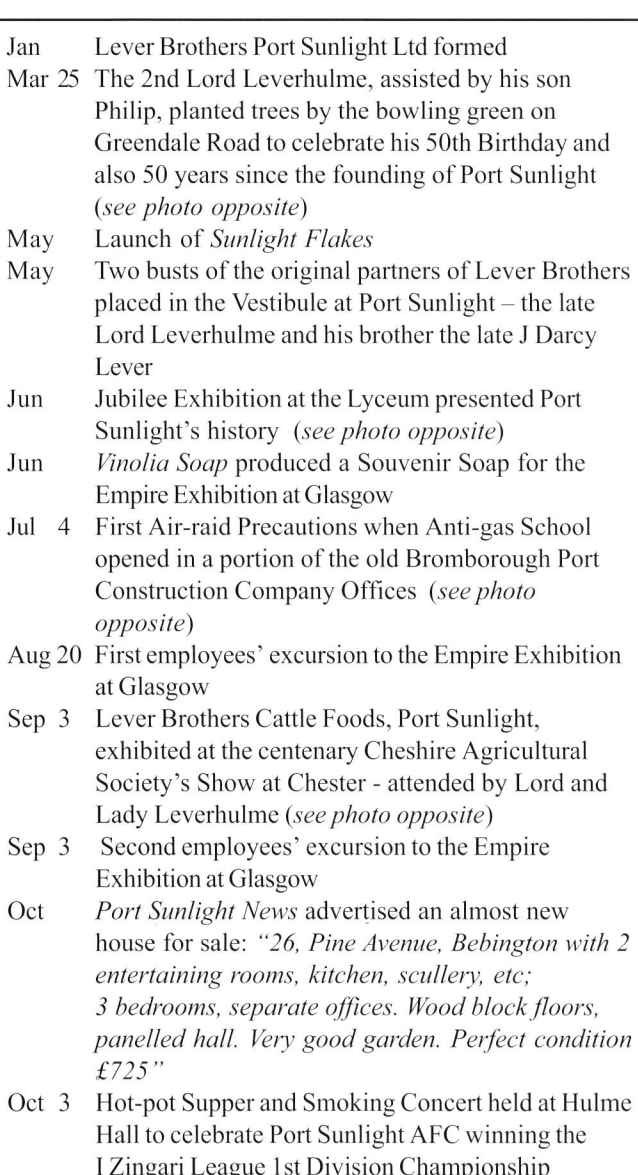

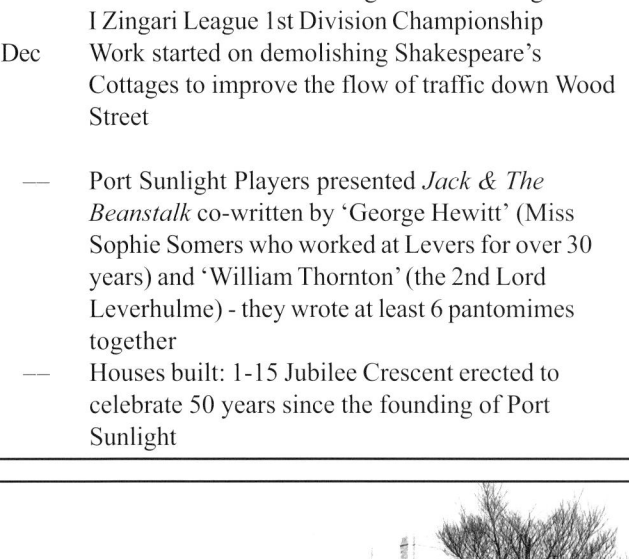

Left: *Seen here under construction, the houses on Jubilee Crescent, named to commemorate the 50th anniversary of the founding of Port Sunlight*

Above: *Seen here in full protective clothing, members of the Company receive training in anti-gas techniques. The courses started on 4 July 1938 in a part of the old Bromborough Port Construction Offices and later moved to a building opposite Port Sunlight Hospital[UNI]*

Above: *On 25 March 1938 Lord Leverhulme, accompanied by hs wife Freda , Lady Leverhulme, and son Philip, planting one of several trees by the bowling green on Greendale Road to celebrate his 50th birthday and also 50 years since the founding of Port Sunlight[UNI]*

Above: *To celebrate Lever Brother's Jubilee at Port Sunlight, an exhibition was held at the Lyceum including relics and souvenirs from Bolton and Warrington which pre-dated Port Sunlight. Some of those present could still remember the arrival of Mr and Mrs Lever at the old stone quay on their way to the site of the No.1 Soapery where Mrs Lever cut the first sod in March 1888[UNI]*

Above: *The Port Sunlight Ladies' Netball Team won the Liverpool Union of Girls First Open Division Shield in 1938 – Standing: L Eastman, A Miles, B Ollerhead, W Webster, E Wilkinson Seated: E Gill, W Miles, L Macpherson[UNI]*

Above: *Lord and Lady Leverhulme were photographed outside the Lever Brothers' Cattle Foods Stand at the Cheshire Agricultural Society's Show held at Chester on 2-3 September 1938. An enterprising Lever's Agent acquired one of the photographs and obtained their signatures which can be seen at the bottom of the picture[UNI]*

Jan 7	Shakespeare's Cottages demolished (see photo)
Feb 23	The 'Lux Lovelies', who performed a special cabaret show at leading Gaumont cinemas throughout the country, visited Port Sunlight (see photo opposite)
Mar	The latest Sunlight Soap offer of a set of six Royal Tudor Ware fruit Dishes, Chatsworth Tapestry design, for only 10 carton fronts plus sixpence postage & packaging, was proving very popular
Apr 26	A demonstration was given of the Air Raid Precautions (ARP) at Port Sunlight (see photo opposite)
Jun	Personnel from Port Sunlight attended the 67th Light Anti-Aircraft Battery, Royal Artillery TA camp at Cark, near Morecambe Bay
Jun	A cheque of £254 was sent from the employees and Company to the Thetis Fund – the Thetis crew had visited Port Sunlight a short time before the submarine sank during sea trials in Liverpool Bay off Anglesey with 99 lives lost
Jun	Advertised in the Port Sunlight News 'For Sale':- Semi-Detached House – 92, St Andrews Road. Spital. Attractive, well-built semi-detached house. Two entertaining rooms, three bedrooms, tiled bathroom and kitchen, large garden, garage. Price £600
Jun 1	Lever Brothers' telephone number changed from Rock Ferry 500 to Rock Ferry 2000
Aug	A few days before the outbreak of war, the Lady Lever Art Gallery was closed to the public and the collection removed to safe storage. It was used throughout the war for exhibitions by the War Office, employees and local societies
Aug	The camping season at Thurstaston came to an abrupt end due to the impending war - it was taken over by the Military and by an Anti-Aircraft Battery, re-opening for a short period after the war
Sep	Port Sunlight Cricket Club first and second teams both topped their respective Divisions in the Merseyside Competition
Sep	Throughout September orders poured in at such a high rate, due to housewives stocking-up, that they had to be rationed
Sep 3	WAR IS DECLARED
Sep	Following the outbreak of war, air raid shelters were built and an ARP organisation started
Sep 18	The late Lord Leverhulme's sister, Miss Emily Lever, of Hesketh Grange, Thornton Hough, died aged 91
Nov 17	First air-raid warning at 11.25am. Evacuation was carried out in an orderly manner with everyone proceeding to their allotted shelters (see photo opposite)
Dec	Over 700 employees at Port Sunlight had joined the forces or some form of National Service since September
Dec	Company War Savings campaign launched
Dec 2	Port Sunlight Allotment Holders' Society was formed with 200 members, the object being bulk purchase of seeds, fertilizers, lime etc for resale to members. Advice was also given on cultivation and treatment of insects and plant diseases
—	Saddle tank locomotive Perfection delivered - renamed Sunlight in March 1940

Above: The happy Company camper portrayed in this cartoon would not realise that the last the 1939 camp would be one of the last as it was soon to be requisitioned by the Military and only opened for a short period after the war. [UNI]

Above: The finished houses in Jubilee Crescent with the ornamental archway, built in 1933, in the foreground [UNI]

Above: Shakespeare's Cottages, built in 1896 on Poets Corner at the bottom of Wood Street, in the process of being demolished [UNI]

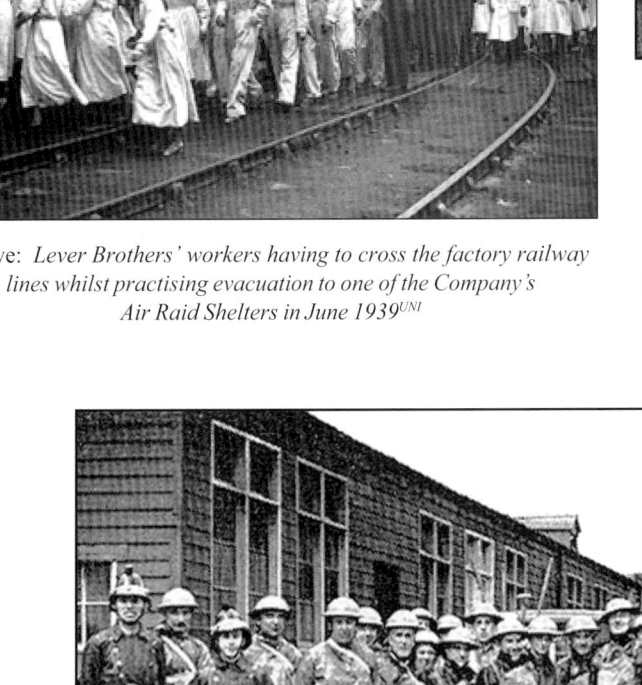

Above: *The use of famous film stars to sell* Lux Soap *started in the 1930s and continued for over 50 years using many famous names. These are some of the 'Lux Lovelies' and their compere photographed in the* Lux *packing department during a visit to Port Sunlight Factory*[UNI]

Above: *Port Sunlight Men's Hockey Club first & second teams posing after an end-of-season friendly in 1939*[UNI]

Above: *Lever Brothers' workers having to cross the factory railway lines whilst practising evacuation to one of the Company's Air Raid Shelters in June 1939*[UNI]

Above: *The ARP volunteers are digging trenches in the village June 1939*[UNI]

Below: *Taken during the ARP demonstration given on 26 April 1939, this shows some of the 30 members of staff who had been trained as Auxiliary Firemen. Over 600 in total had been trained at the Company's ARP School*[UNI]

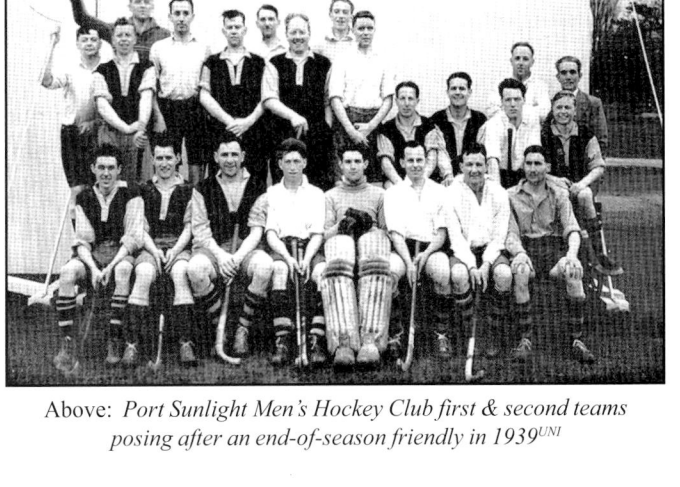

1940

1940

Jan	Port Sunlight National Savings Group was formed
Jan	The worst snowstorms in living memory
Jan 6	First wartime concert given by Port Sunlight Players with proceeds to the local branch of the Women's Wartime Sewing Parties
Jan 27	Exhibition of Art held at Lady Lever Art Gallery presenting works by employees at Port Sunlight and Unilever House including paintings, drawings, sculpture, handicraft and needlework. There was also an Exhibition of Works by members of the Birkenhead Photographic Association
Feb	The site of a proposed new stadium and club premises at Bromborough was put under the plough for the 'Dig for Victory' campaign - [the Stadium was never built, but Stadium Road was built and still runs behind the cinema complex on the Bromborough Business Park – see 1951]
Feb 22	First lecture "Allotment Management in Wartime" given to the Port Sunlight Allotment Holders' Society
Mar	To help war rationing of paper, Port Sunlight News was reduced to 24 pages
Mar 2	Funds raised from the performance of Lot's Wife by the Port Sunlight Players went towards the Red Cross and Comforts Fund (see poster opposite)
Apr	A nine-hole putting green was opened on the Port Sunlight Golf Club Course
May	The Bebington Borough Area LDV (Local Defence Volunteers) was formed with over 1,200 men who were mostly ex-service – the LDV later became the Home Guard
May 22	War Savings Campaign Port Sunlight Group 'Thermometer' exhibited at the factory entrance (see photo)
Jun	No.4 Wirral Battalion (later the 21st Battalion Cheshire Home Guard) was formed
Jun 15	Nurses Home opened at Port Sunlight opposite the Hospital at the corner of Central Road and Lodge Lane (see photos)
Jun 15	An exhibition of photographs of "Our Forces in The Field" opened for 2 weeks at the Lady Lever Art Gallery
Jul	'E' Company in 21st Battalion Cheshire Home Guard (factory unit) was formed with 500 men
Jul 1	Royal Warrants were granted to Lever Brothers Port Sunlight and to the Vinolia Co Ltd as Soapmakers to His Majesty King George VI
Aug	There were 390 allotments under cultivation on the Company's estates, a third of them being new since October 1939
Aug	Direct war work started with the manufacture of small parts and the reconditioning of blitzed machine tools from firms on Merseyside and elsewhere
Aug 20	Lever Bros & Unilever Ltd together with their employees funded a Bomber for Britain at a cost of £20,000
Sep 21	The Port Sunlight Boys' Brigade returned from Bromyard in Staffordshire where they were employed for a week in picking hops and potatoes
Oct 17/18	Severe damage caused to Port Sunlight village during an air raid. Three killed at 55 Pool Bank

Nov 16 A fully equipped Mobile Canteen was presented by Lord & Lady Leverhulme to the County of Cheshire – it was kept at the new Police Station at Bromborough and served the Borough of Bebington

(see photo opposite)

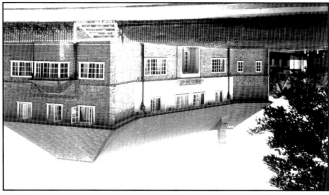

Above: The nurses home on the corner of Lodge Lane and Central Road was opened on 15 June 1940 UNI

Above: Seen here at the opening of the Nurses' Home: Mr & Mrs Briggs, their daughter Gillian and the Matron (Miss Anderson) accompanied Lord & Lady Leverhulme, Mr & Mrs Joseph Wainwright, Mr AW Henry, Mr & Mrs FS Walker, Mr & Mrs R McLean, Mr FA Lawman and members of the nursing staff UNI

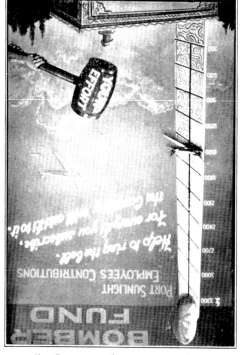

Right: This 10ft. x 7ft. poster was displayed by the works' main gate showing progress of the 'Bomber Fund' week-by-week UNI

Above: *This Junkers JU88 crash landed near Bromborough Pool Village on 8 October 1940. One of the crew was killed. The other three, of whom two were injured, were 'captured' by two company employees, Harry Gill and Rob Thompson, before being handed over to the authorities. After removal of any sensitive military items, the bomber was taken to Port Sunlight Recreation Ground and put on display to the public, raising more than £70 for the 'Mayor of Bebington's Spitfire Fund'*[UNI]

GLADSTONE HALL
PORT SUNLIGHT

Saturday, 2nd March, 1940

PORT SUNLIGHT PLAYERS
will present

LOT'S WIFE

A Modern Comedy in Three Acts
By PETER BLACKMORE

Doors Open at 7 p.m.   Commence at 7-30 p.m.

The proceeds are in aid of

✚

Red Cross and Comforts Funds
(Mayoress of Bebington's Appeal)

TICKETS : 2/- and 1/-

From:
Mr. McWilliam, Service Department, Lever
Brothers, Port Sunlight, Limited
Tel. Rock Ferry 2000, Extn. 315

Miss E. Somers, Lever Free Library, Greendale
Road, Port Sunlight.
Tel. Rock Ferry 2000, Extn. 324

Or from any member of the Port Sunlight Players

SEATS WILL BE RESERVED AT NO EXTRA CHARGE
By arrangement with Mr. McWilliam

● **PLEASE BOOK EARLY** ●

UNI

Right: *The Mobile Canteen, presented by Lord & Lady Leverhulme to Chester County Council, is seen here outside Bromborough Police Station*[UNI]

Right: *Many parts of the village were turned over to food production. This area near to the Bridge Inn was grassland less than 12 months before*[UNI]

Above: *Members of the Port Sunlight Golf Club pose for a photograph on the occasion of the opening of the new putting green. In the background on the right is the former Vinolia building, and on the left is the golf clubhouse*[UNI]

Above: *Port Sunlight Old Boys' AFC pictured in March 1940*[UNI]

Above: *Lever Brothers were awarded several Government War Contracts which included an order for 10,000 tank periscopes which are being assembled here* UNI

Above: *Another view of Tank Periscopes being assembled* UNI

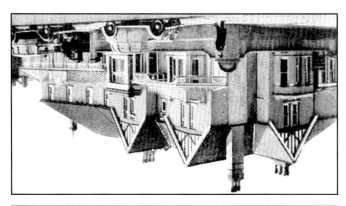

Above: Sandringham, Levers' holiday home at Llandudno, where many employees were able to escape for some rest and quiet during the war years UNI

Bath Units which were both self-contained and could operate where water or heating facilities had been cut off. By 1944 an estimated 3.25 million garments had been washed and over 1,000,000 people had received showers (*see photo opposite*)

— Government war contracts included 1,000,000 paper cylinders for 25 pounder shells; heater pipes and curtains for Wellington bombers; 10,000 tank periscopes and massage oil for use at sea in lifeboats (*see photos*)

Jan	Lever Brothers purchased a large house *Sandringham* in Llandudno as a place for their employees and families who were suffering from 'war strain' or the effects of the bombing to go for a holiday (*see photo*)
Mar 6	The Boys' Cadet Division of the Port Sunlight St John Ambulance Brigade held its first meeting at the Corps Headquarters on New Chester Road for boys aged between 11 & 17
Mar 12/13	A land-mine destroyed 14-18 Bolton Road, 8-14 Bridge Street, the Collegium and the Employees' Provident Stores (MacFisheries) - which quickly re-opened in the Gymnasium). Many houses in the village were damaged
Apr	Lady Lever Art Gallery exhibited a First World War Exhibition loaned by the Imperial War Museum
Jul 22	The Maternity Home at Bromborough Pool was closed due to structural damage caused by bombing - later moved to new premises at *Heathfield* on Croft Avenue Bromborough
Aug 25	Port Sunlight launched their £20,000 War Savings Campaign to supply a tank
Sep	Arthur Askey paid a visit to Port Sunlight, entertaining an enthusiastic crowd in the Girls' Dining Hall and also promoted the various War Savings projects
Sep	Final amount raised in 3 months by the War Savings Campaign for a Tank was over £25,800 which was enough to purchase several tanks (*see photo opposite*)
Sep 2	The start of the 'Bebington Garden Front and Dig for Victory Week' which was held in the Hulme Hall — the varied programme throughout the week included: a cookery demonstration, a Victory Garden Show, a film entitled "A Garden Goes to War" and other related topics
Sep 20	An Allied Artists Exhibition was opened for a month at the Lady Lever Art Gallery
Oct 29	George Formby entertained employees in the Girls' Dining Hall, and at the end of his performance he congratulated the workers on their War Savings Campaign
Nov	Saddle tank locomotive *Barry* arrived at Port Sunlight – initially hired then purchased and rebuilt in 1946
Nov 14	Another entertainer, Will Fyffe, the Scottish comedian and film star, performed at lunch-time in the Girls' Dining Hall and ended by congratulating the workers on their War Saving Campaigns
Dec 15	Launch of the latest Port Sunlight War Savings Drive with the target £30,000 to buy 1 Wellington Bomber and 2 Hurricane Fighters
Dec 18	The death was announced of Sir F D'Arcy Cooper, Bt, the Chairman of Lever Bros & Unilever Ltd
Dec	Return visit during Christmas Week of George Formby to entertain the workers and help the Aeroplane Drive
—	Levers made available two emeregency services each consisting of a fleet of huge vans which were built and equipped at Port Sunlight - Laundry Units and

Working at Port Sunlight During the War

Norman Tomlinson in his book *Walking Through The Blitz* in *the Birkenhead area* recalls as a 17 year-old reporting for work at the offices of Unilever Export Limited, Port Sunlight on the morning after the raid on the 12/13 March 1941 "On 14 March I was back at the office at Port Sunlight and found that everyone had spent 13 March clearing up there. A large bomb (land mine) had landed about 150 yards away destroying Mac Fisheries' Bakery near the bowling green. The blast from the bomb had caused a lot of damage to the office roof and smashed a great deal of glass. Many years later that roof leaked every time it rained".

And of the 'May Blitz' [1-7 May 1941] he writes:

"'…To avoid total loss of the buses it had become the practice at Laird Street Bus Depot to disperse them each night around Birkenhead Park (the steering wheel of each bus was removed as it was still necessary to ensure that any parked vehicle was made immobile in event of invasion). Despite this however many buses were destroyed or damaged and I found myself riding to the office at Port Sunlight on buses without any windows or without a roof. It was still a bit chilly in the morning with the wind whipping around one's hands and feet'.

Above: *This kiosk manned by two of the Port Sunlight Guides was just one of the many campaigns to encourage Port Sunlight employees to support the drive to raise funds during the war. The Company cleverly used their name in LeVer to highlight the 'V' in Lever to associate it with Churchill's V for Victory sign* [UNI]

Left: *Areas within the factory were set aside for war production – girls can be seen packing war rations for the troops* [UNI]

Above: *This Compo Pack for the troops was one of many assembled at Port Sunlight* [UNI]

Left: *Two men are helping to clear this bombed building in Port Sunlight following air raids* [UNI]

Above: *Lifebuoy Mobile Bathing Units originally supplied to provide bathing facilities for troops but brought into service for members of the public whose homes had been destroyed by enemy action in London* [UNI]

1942

Jan 14   Tommy Handley, the well known comedian and radio star drew a large audience at the Girls' Dining Hall encouraging the workers to help the Savings Drive

Feb   Total for the Aeroplane Drive was £41,696 - enough to buy a Wellington Bomber and 4 Hurricane Fighters

Feb   The Ladies Page of *Port Sunlight News* gave the following 'Make Do & Mend' tip: *A woollen jumper that is badly worn under the armholes, and perhaps at the elbows, can be made into a very warm and useful pair of knickers for a toddler or schoolchild*

Feb 8   Soap rationing introduced which cut production and released space and manpower for war work

Feb 11   Mr Jack Train, stage and radio star, visited Port Sunlight to entertain the workers

Feb 25   A Girls' Cadet Nursing Division for girls between 14 & 16, was formed and attached to the Port Sunlight Division of the Port Sunlight Corps

Mar   The number of allotments increased to 422

Mar   Tribute was paid to the Works' Fireguard and ARP whose prompt and efficient action had prevented any major damage to the factory by the large numbers of incendiary bombs which had fallen on Port Sunlight

Mar 7   The week-long exhibition of weapons commenced at Lady Lever Art Gallery in conjunction with the Bebington Warship Week – admittance was by buying a 6d War Savings Stamp - a total of £1,871 was raised by the exhibition

Mar 9   Prince Bernhard of the Netherlands visited the Port Sunlight works

Apr 20   Port Sunlight appealed to all employees to 'Wage a Campaign Against Waste' through a feature in the *Port Sunlight News* and posters throughout the factory and offices

May 30   End of the Anti-Waste and Salvage Drive at Port Sunlight which resulted in 209 tons of waste paper – enough for 313,500 shell containers: 272 tons of iron & steel – enough for 14 tanks or 27,000 Bren guns: 55 cwts of rubber – sufficient to equip 35 Churchill Tanks, and 35 cwts of hessian and twine – would make more than 2 miles length of fire hose for the NFS (National Fire Service)

Jun   Work began in No.2 Soapery to pack forces rations

Jun   The Wirral Grammar School Arts Festival was held at the Lady Lever Art Gallery

Jun 3   King Haakon of Norway and Crown Prince Olav visited works

Aug 19   Will Fyffe returned to entertain the workers at Port Sunlight bringing with him Beryl Reid and the Dagenham Girl Pipers

Sep   The Womens' Page of the *Port Sunlight News* gave a recipe for 'Parsley Wine', 'Carrot Marmalade' and hints on how to make elastic last twice as long!

Sep 21   Male hairdressing facilities started in the factory at a charge of one shilling

Sep 25   New canteen opened at Bromborough Dock by the Mersey Docks and Harbour Board described as "the Ritz of all Merseyside Canteens"

Oct 17   Rev Horace Wright, Minister at Thornton Hough

1942

Congregational Church, appointed as Minister at Christ Church for the duration of the war and for 12 months afterwards - with an assistant Minister to be appointed (*see photo*)

Oct   The 99th concert in the 'BBC Works Wonders' series was broadcast from the Girls' Dining Hall Port Sunlight

Nov 30   Over £50,000 saved for the Motor Torpedo Boat Drive

—   US Army vehicles from Dodge jeeps to giant Dodge trucks arrived in huge cases by sea – they were assembled at Port Sunlight and eventually helped in the North African campaign (*see photo on page 95*)

—   The 'Dowry Department' - the biggest engineering undertaking at Port Sunlight - was set up in the Printing Department to manufacture the retractable under-carriages for Lancaster bombers which were designed by George Dowty (*see photo*)

—   The 2nd Bebington Air Training Corps Squadron were asking for recruits from Port Sunlight

Above: Retractable under-carriages for Lancaster bombers, which were designed by George Dowty, are seen being assembled in the 'Dowry Department' - the biggest engineering undertaking at Port Sunlight – which was set up in the Printing Department

Right: The Rev Horace W Wright, Minister of St George's Congregational Church at Thornton Hough, who also took on the position of Minister of Christ Church, Port Sunlight for the duration of the war

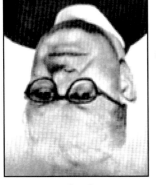

Below: Seen here is the purpose-built research building opened in Port Sunlight in 1942. In the background on the right is the former Vinolia building, and to the left the Port Sunlight Golf course UNI

Feb	First Lancaster bomber undercarriages produced at Port Sunlight left the factory
Mar 8	'Wings for Victory' War Savings Drive to save £30,000 for a squadron of 6 Spitfires launched at Port Sunlight
Mar 14	Rev Charles L Storer appointed as Assistant to Rev Horace W Wright, Minister of Christ Church Port Sunlight (*see photo*)
May	A further Royal Air Force Exhibition was displayed at the Lady Lever Art Gallery in connection with the 'Wings for Victory' War Savings Drive using a series of photographic enlargements supplied by the Ministry of Information - representing the work of Coastal Command, Air Rescue at Sea, the making of bombs, the work of Bomber Command, the Fleet Air Arm and phases of air fighting in every sector of the war - the selling centre at the gallery exceeded all previous war efforts with a collection amounting to £3,790
May 23	Annual Red Cross Cricket Match with a Port Sunlight XI (with 50% players from Oxton, Birkenhead etc) versus a Learie Constantine XI (50% West Indians & 50% from Bootle)
Jul 3	'Wings for Victory' Drive brought in £42,327 against a target of £30,000 - this amount was enough to purchase 8 Spitfires
Jul 15	A 10-day exhibition of pictures depicting 'The RAF on Target' commenced at the Lady Lever Art Gallery
Aug 14	Port Sunlight Boys' Brigade went down to Evesham in Worcestershire for their annual camp where they helped in the harvesting of the fruit orchards and also helping local farmers with more arduous tasks
Sep 7	The Port Sunlight Male Voice Choir was established - originally known as the 'Gladstone Singers', who started by singing in air-raid shelters, then 12 of them banded together and gave concerts to cheer the sick and wounded
Sep/Oct	The *Port Sunlight News* 'Women's Notes' related a 'Make Do And Mend' Exhibition where one of the ladies wore a trim navy blue coat and skirt which had been made from her husband's suit!
Nov 12	The Girls' Dining Hall was the venue for a 'welcome home' party for two repatriated prisoners-of-war . Their message from the soldiers who were still prisoners was to continue helping the Red Cross - without their parcels the majority of prisoners would not have survived
—	Production of *Lux Flakes* stopped due to shortages of raw materials
—	The Boys' Brigade were advised of vacancies in the local company of the Home Guard, for boys between 16 and 17 years of age, for inter-communication duties - with parental consent essential!

Above: *Even the rose beds in The Diamond were turned over to help feed the residents of Port Sunlight. To the left of the child in the foreground is a sign which says: "Please keep off plots sown with vegetables"*[UNI]

Above: *The Rev Charles Leonard Storer was appointed assistant to the Rev Wright, Minister of Christ Church, in 1943*

Right: *This was an advert for a specially produced 'Service Pack' of* Vinolia[UNI] *products – an ideal Christmas present for a man in the forces*

Right: *Pre-war* Rinso *demonstration vans which were first used after the air raids on Wallasey. They were in-effect mobile laundries complete with emergency water tanks, washing machines, sinks, drying cabinets etc. By July 1943 there was a fleet of 10 covering all Merseyside and had been extended to London*[UNI]

Below: *The Officers and Sergeants of the 21st 'E' Company of the Cheshire Home Guard photographed in Port Sunlight after a Sunday morning training parade*[UNI]

Mar 27 'Salute the Soldier' War Savings Campaign was launched - it was hoped to raise £50,000 to buy eight 5.5 guns

Apr 28 An American 'Duck' landing craft and a smaller 'Peep' were on display at Port Sunlight to raise funds for the 'Salute the Soldier Week' and anyone purchasing a savings stamp could write a message on the craft

May Volunteers were once again requested to take Holidays on the land to help out with planting and harvesting of crops in Cheshire, Staffordshire and Cumberland - the rate of pay was 1 shilling per hour

May Several dances and variety shows were arranged for the entertainment of American Forces

May 20 Miss Alice Lever, the eldest surviving sister of the late Lord Leverhulme died at her home Hesketh Grange, Thornton Hough, aged 94

Jul 10 Start of a 'Make Do and Mend' Exhibition and Mannequin Parade held in the Office Annex (adjacent to No.2 Woodbox and Postal department)

Jul 28 'Salute the Soldier' raised £51,471 of savings – enough to buy the eight 5.5 inch guns hoped for

Dec 3 Stand Down of the 21st Cheshire (Bebington) Battalion Home Guard and the 214th (102nd Cheshire Home Guard - AA Battery) was taken outside the Lady Lever Art Gallery (see photo opposite)

— During 1944 Bromborough Dock handled one-eighth of all Mersey maritime traffic

— Saddle tank locomotive *Bromport*, built in 1868 and the oldest locomotive to have worked for Lever Brothers, purchased second-hand from Broomside Colliery in Scotland

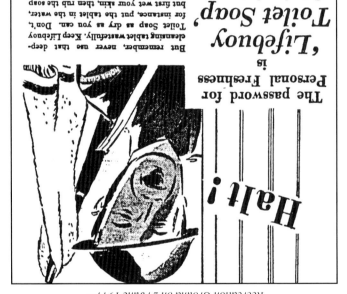

Above: *A wartime Lifebuoy Toilet Soap*[UNI] *advert*

Above: *Seen here in ATS uniform, The Princess Royal with the Mayor and Mayoress of Bebington (Alderman & Mrs AW Eaton), the Lord Lieutenant of Cheshire (Sir W Bromley-Davenport), Lord Leverhulme, and other dignitaries at a Youth Rally held at the Port Sunlight Recreation Ground on 24 June 1944*[UNI]

Above: *These War Savings Collectors were refered to by Lord Leverhulme during the opening of the 'Salute the Soldier' campaign, in the following terms:* "They are the spearhead of our campaign and if you can say 'no' to them when they ask you to buy a certificate, then you are a very obdurate person indeed"[UNI]

Above: *The 'Stand-Down' parade of the Bebington Home Guard was held on 3 December 1944. The salute was taken by Lieut. Col. NA Willis, Commandant of the Western Command Weapon Training School, accompanied by the Mayor of Bebington, Lord Leverhulme and Colonel Briggs*[UNI]

Port Sunlight Employees' War Appeals Fund.

The Committee regret that it has not been found possible to proceed with the idea of sending periodicals to those employees who have expressed a preference for this form of gift. Owing to the limitation of supplies, the publishers now inform us that they will be unable to provide the extra copies required.

The Committee are sorry they are unable to carry out your wishes in this respect, but feel sure that you will appreciate the position.

With best wishes,
J. R. JOHNSON,
(Secretary)

Above: *This wartime postcard appears to have been sent to employees in the Services who had requested copies of the* Port Sunlight News *but couldn't have them due to shortages of paper, especially towards the end of the war*

Above: *Detachments of the Port Sunlight Fire Brigade and Works Fire Guard which took part in the 'Salute the Soldier' Parade at Bebington on 22 April 1944 were as follows:*
Left to right (front row): RC Davies, W Hayes, RH Davies, E Davies, JJ Smith & T Williams: (2nd row): L/Fireman Greenwood, Firemen Langford & Marsh, Major PGH Broadhurst, Colonel E Briggs, W Price, Firemen Lewis, Donnelly & Barclay (3rd row): L Klaces, H Carr, W Webster, JH Coombes, M Fitzpatrick G Bather, SC Jones, E Williams, T Williams & RC Hill (back row): J Bedrock, T Hozack, J Dyson, C Boulton, CC Dunn, S West, M Cogan, J Taylor & RH Fletcher[UNI]

Above: *These left-hand drive army trucks, seen awaiting despatch outside the Printing Department in the Port Sunlight Factory, were sent over from America in parts and assembled here*

Feb 1   Port Sunlight at War Exhibition opens (*see photos opposite*)

Feb 20   Over £500,000 of War Savings had been raised at Port Sunlight

Mar   Members of the Mobile Emergency Services left for Holland with their vehicles (*see photo*)

May   The Lady Lever Art Gallery exhibits were returned home to Port Sunlight from their war-home in North Wales

May 6   Colours presented to the Bebington Unit of the Women's Junior Air Corps outside Christ Church Port Sunlight (*see photo*)

May 8   Hulme Hall was overflowing with an excited crowd celebrating Victory In Europe Day and the company paid all the expenses! The village was bedecked with flags & bunting with several bonfires being lit, and many street parties, enjoyed especially by the children

Jul   Due to heavy rain the basement of the Lady Lever Art Gallery was flooded

Jul 2   New War Savings Drive opened to raise £25,000 to buy a Medical Unit for use in the Far East

Aug 15   VJ (Victory in Japan) Day was celebrated in Port Sunlight with many parties held especially for the children

Sep 29   A 'Make Do and Mend' Exhibition held in Hulme Hall - although the war was over, rationing was worse than ever

Sep 29   Employees' War Appeals Fund closed

Oct 5   The warship *Icarus,* with submarines *Truculent* and *Seneschal* berthed in Bromborough Dock for an official visit (*see photo opposite*)

Oct 8   Port Sunlight Girls' Club was re-opened for its normal peace-time activities having been used as a First Aid Post during the war

Oct 27   2nd Lord Leverhulme became the First Freeman of Bebington

Nov 6   "Lifebuoy Follies" from Canada visited Port Sunlight (*see photo opposite*)

Nov 17   Children's VJ Party held in the main hall of Church Drive Junior School

Above: *Three members of the Decontamination Service: From Lt. to Rt.: Mr A Broxton, Mr J Birkett, Mr W Abel who were selected to represent the Admiralty Contract Firms in the North-West Region at the Civil Defence Farewell Parade in Hyde Park, London, before King George VI on 10 June 1945*[UNI]

Above: *Seen here outside Christ Church Port Sunlight after being presented with their new colours by Lord & Lady Leverhulme, are members of the Bebington and Birkenhead Units of the Women's Junior Air Corps*[UNI]

Below: *Members of the Mobile Emergency Services seen here with Lord Leverhulme and the Chairman Mr Briggs, before leaving for Holland with their vehicles in March 1945*[UNI]

Above: Visitors receive a 'helping hand' aboard one of the submarines, during their visit to Bromborough Dock in October – whilst a group of young men man the guns! (UNI)

Below: The Lifebuoy goods train halts for a moment during a journey through the Works to form an appropriate background for the photograph of the Canadian 'Lifebuoy Follies' during their visit to the Port Sunlight Factory seen here with the Chairman Mr E Briggs (UNI)

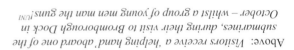

Above and Below Right: The 'Port Sunlight at War' exhibition was held in the Lyceum to illustrate the amazing range of direct war work carried out in the Port Sunlight factory since the outbreak of war.

Feb 25	Introduction of two-weeks paid holiday by the Company
Mar	War Exhibition, moved from the Lyceum into the factory, continued to display items processed or packed by the Company during the war years (*see photo*)
May	Work commenced on Bromborough Power Station (*see photo*)
May 1	The Men's Club arranged Exhibition Billiards and Snooker matches between 2 world-renowned players - Horace Lindrum and Sydney Smith - watched by over 400 members at the Lyceum
May 13	Introduction of five-day week into offices – 8.30am to 5.30pm. No Saturdays and afternoon tea provided free
May 19	Empire Youth Sunday Pageant for the Bebington District started from the Lady Lever Art Gallery and the 500 youths, including 1st Port Sunlight Company Boys' Brigade, marched to Christ Church via Primrose Hill (*see photo*)
May/Jun	*Port Sunlight News* 'Women's Notes' included economy recipes: *Chocolate Potato Buns* and *Potato Parkins* under the heading "Potatoey But Nice"
Jun 1	Thurstaston Holiday Camp re-opened for the season
Jun 3	The Ladies' Cricket Club AGM was the first to be held since 1939
Jun 8	The Company was well represented at the Victory Parade in London
Jun 16	Miss Harriet Lever, the 1st Lord Leverhulme's sister, died at Thornton Hough, aged 91
Sep 21	Thurstaston Camp closed for the season
—	Rev Charles L Storer - Assistant Minister of Christ Church - announced his departure having been at Port Sunlight since 1943
—	Former Central Technical Department renamed The Research Department

Above: *Empire Youth Sunday took place on 19 May when over 500 young people representing youth organisations in Bebington assembled at the Art Gallery before the 'march past' and service at Christ Church*[UNI]

Above: *The Central Electricity Power Station under construction at Bromborough with the Stork Margerine Factory in the background*[UNI]

Above: *The Engineering Department won the 'Soap Bowl' in the mixed Inter-Group Hockey Competition. Lt. to Rt. Back row: WF Smith, A Peers, A Gooding, WE Davies, A Webster, T Yeardsley Front row: D Reed, B Green, K Ware, E Price*[UNI]

Above: *The War Exhibition originally held in the Lyceum, re-located to Central Road inside the factory, continued to display items made at Port Sunlight in support of the war effort*[UNI]

Right: *Lieut. Col. Ernest Briggs CBE DSO who retired at the end of the year after eight years as Chairman of Lever Brothers*[UNI]

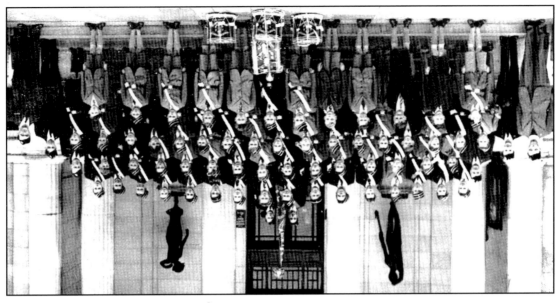

Above: The 'Vivos' were the Concert Party section of the Port Sunlight Players. From Lt. to Rt.: Miss Grace Whiteside, Mr Stan Spencer, Miss Pat Bennett, Mr Johnny Bridges (Producer), Mr Ernie Dawkin, Mr Len Weaver (Chairman), Mrs Eve Tate, Miss Alice Smith and Miss Enid Smith, Mrs Dot Weaver, Pianist[UNI]

Right: The winning Bebington 'B', team in the Rotary Trophy Competition for Nursing and Ambulance Cadets of the Port Sunlight Corps of St John Ambulance Brigade[UNI]

Below: The 1st Port Sunlight Company of the Boys' Brigade pictured on Empire Youth Sunday with their Chaplain, the Rev Charles L Storer[UNI]

Rebuilding works gets underway following bomb damage to houses in Port Sunlight Village[UNI]

Jan 1 Mr GAS Nairn appointed Chairman of Lever Brothers (*see photo*)

Feb 10 Port Sunlight Factory partly shut when coal shortage led to electricity cuts

Mar 3 Introduction of 42-hour week in Port Sunlight factory

Mar 11 Rev George Markham inducted as Minister of Christ Church Port Sunlight (*see photo*)

May Job evaluation scheme introduced by Lever Brothers

Jul 16 Luncheon & Reception at the Lady Lever Art Gallery to celebrate the Silver Jubilee of its opening

Oct 1 Union Pension scheme replaces Provident Fund

Nov *Lux Flakes* sales re-commenced having been withdrawn in 1943

Nov 9 Dedication of 1939-45 tablet on War Memorial

— Purchase of a new grab-hopper dredger *Sand Swallow II* to replace the original *Sand Swallow*. Although the Westminster Dredging Company raised most of the silt, their vessels could not be used close to the quays or the lock entrance, but the *Sand Swallow* could (*see photo*) – the new dredger disposed of 33,000 cubic yards of silt every year

— Bowling Green by Lyceum constructed on the former tennis courts

— Short-time working because of fuel crisis

— Port Sunlight AFC West Cheshire AF League Champions 1946/47

— Houses rebuilt or refurbished following war damage: 99-109 Bebington Road; 14-18 Bolton Road; 1-11 Boundary Road; 8-14 Bridge Street; 8-13 Church Drive and 19, 31-35 & 55 Pool Bank

How to cope without clipping coupons

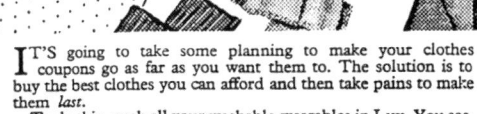

IT'S going to take some planning to make your clothes coupons go as far as you want them to. The solution is to buy the best clothes you can afford and then take pains to make them *last*.

To do this, wash all your washable wearables in Lux. You see, Lux˙dissolves in lukewarm water and only low-temperature washing is safe if you want delicate fabrics to last. And with Lux you don't need to rub. The lather is so rich that a quick squeeze-through makes things brilliantly clean.

Start with Lux today, and even your finest undies will last and last. It's grand to know that Lux is still pre-war price and weight.

LUX MAKES CLOTHES LAST

A *LEVER* PRODUCT

Above: This Lux^UNI Advert followed the re-commencement of Lux Flakes production which had stopped due to shortages of raw materials in 1943. Clothes coupons were introduced on 2 June 1941 and rationing ended March 1949

Left: *Mr GAS Nairn who was appointed Chairman of Lever Brothers in 1947 in succession to Col. Briggs^UNI*

Right: *Re-building work was completed on 8-14 Bridge Street following bomb damage suffered during the war*

Left: *The Rev George Markham who was appointed Minister of Christ Church Port Sunlight in March 1947*

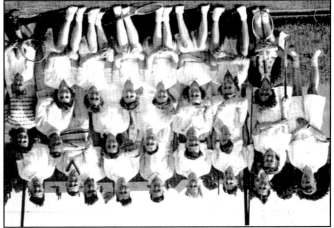

Above: Members of the 1947 Port Sunlight Lawn Tennis Club. In the Club Handicap Tournaments, Miss Beryl Price won the Ladies' Singles. In the Doubles, Miss Sheila Davies & Miss Amy Paull won the Ladies', Mr RJ Behan & Mr WF Smith the Men's, and Mr & Mrs TP Williams won the Mixed^UNI

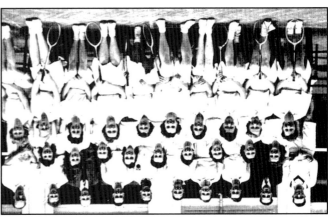

Above: The 1947 Port Sunlight Badminton Club whose League Team were undefeated in all 10 of their matches this season^UNI

Above: Loading cases onto a vessel in Bromborough Dock^UNI

Above: The 'Lux Washability Bureau' stand at the British Industries Fair on 5 May 1947 with Miss Barbara Towle, head of the Bureau in the centre^UNI

Above: Sand Swallow II delivered in 1947 to replace the original Sand Swallow which had been in operation since 1924 keeping the tidal creek and docks clear of mud and sand^UNI

Feb	Service in Christ Church to celebrate The Diamond Jubilee of Port Sunlight
Feb 19	Diesel Locomotive *Princess Elizabeth* delivered to Port Sunlight
Apr 6	Diesel Locomotive *Princess Margaret* delivered to Port Sunlight
May 15	Opening of the Merseyside's Festival of Sport Week held at the Recreation Grounds at Bebington (*see photo*)
Jul 5	Sickness and Industrial Benefit scheme introduced
Aug	Manufacture commenced in No.3 Soapery of the soapless liquid washer *Quix*. The introductory price was two shillings per bottle, later reduced to 1/6d (7.5p) (*see photo opposite*)
Oct 5	2nd Lord Leverhulme opened the Lever Library Extension (*see photo*)
Dec 4	Christmas Fair held at Hulme Hall in aid of Christ Church Organ Restoration Fund opened by 2nd Lord Leverhulme
Dec 20	New system of Joint Consultation launched at Port Sunlight
—	Lever Brothers Area Committees and Consultation Council formed
—	Good Housekeeping and Safety Competitions introduced
—	Port Sunlight AFC won the Pyke Cup and the 2nd Division Championship in the West Cheshire Association Football League 1947/48

Above: *The Rt. Hon. Viscount Leverhulme planting a tree alongside the bowling green on Greendale Road to commemorate the 60th anniversary of the founding of Port Sunlight*[UNI]

Above: *The Port Sunlight Wheelers checking a map before setting off to spend Easter weekend in Caernarvon*[UNI]

Above: *Lord Leverhulme, in the centre of the picture, at the opening of the Lever Library extension watched by the Mayor of Bebington on the left, Freda, Lady Leverhulme and Mr Nairn, Chairman of LeverBrothers on the right*[UNI]

Right: *A Bottle of Quix*[UNI]*, the new soapless washing liquid washer launched in 1948. Advertising claimed it could be used on china, glass, fine fabrics & woollens, windows, paintwork, tiles and cars!*

Left: *An exciting finish to the Five Mile Cycle Race at the Recreation Grounds on the occasion of the opening events of Merseyside's Festival of Sport which ran from the 15 to 22 May 1948*[UNI]

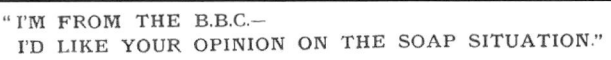

Above: *Mrs Emma Gill, seen here with Lord Leverhulme and Mr Nairn following the tree-planting ceremony, who as a 10 year-old girl witnessed the 'cutting of the first sod' by Mrs Lever in March 1888*[UNI]

Above: *A comic postcard sent in 1948 when 'soap rationing' was still in force. It was 1950 before restrictions were lifted*

Above: *The Bowls Section of the Men's Club who were winners of both the "A" and "B" Divisions of the Bebington Amateur Bowling League amd winners of the Leverhulme Challenge Cup*[UNI]

Above: *Packing* Quix *in 1948 in its distinctive brown glass bottles*[UNI]

Right: *The Port Sunlight Rugby Club 1st XV pictured in 1948 Standing Lt. to Rt.:- WE Clarke,(Hon. Secretary), C Thompson, B Phillips, E Kay, WA Pritchard, D Coathup, RE Dawson, D Reeve, P Cearns, JE Chivers Seated:- D Campbell, R Appleton, T Newby, A Lee, JB Davies, RW Ramsden*[UNI]

Right: *Port Sunlight Fire Brigade in 1948 outside the Fire Station behind the Lever Free Library on Greendale Road*[UNI]

1949

Jan 1 — Wage stability scheme introduced at Port Sunlight

Feb 14 — Co-ordinating Council at Port Sunlight - 2nd meeting discussed company policy over employment of married women – in all cases preference was given to unmarried women with only a few exceptions where it was not always possible

Mar — Port Sunlight Fencing Club formed - meeting fortnightly in the Mens' Dining Hall

May 4 — The new Bus Terminus alongside No.1 Soapery at Port Sunlight was opened by the Minister of Transport

May 27 — **Death of William Hulme Lever,** the 2nd Viscount Leverhulme in America on his way back from a business trip to Australia. His son Philip William Bryce Lever became the 3rd Lord Leverhulme

Jun 25 — First rally for the newly-formed Motor-Cycling Club at Port Sunlight (*see photo opposite*)

Sep 6 — Announcement that the 3rd Viscount Leverhulme had been appointed Lord Lieutenant of Cheshire

Sep 22 — Foundation stone laid for the new Oil Mill on the Bromborough Port Estate

Dec — Port Sunlight Table-Tennis Club formed - meetings held in the Men's Dining Hall

— Port Sunlight AFC won the West Cheshire Bowl

— Company Medical services extended and centralised

— First building to be completed since the war was the Flakes Sub-station near No.3 Soapery

— Royal Coat-of-Arms restored to its position above the factory's main entrance having been taken down and stored away at the beginning of the war (*see photo opposite*)

Above: Virtually the only remaining visible evidence of the tidal creeks which once divided Port Sunlight Village, this peaceful scene in The Dell illustrates how it appeared for many years before it was land-scaped in 1955 using stone from the Company's quarry at Gwernymynydd.[UN]

Above: A portrait of the second Lord Leverhulme who died in 1949

Above: The 1949 final of the Netball Club's Knock-out tournament was won by the No.3 Soapery Flakes Packing Team. They were from Lt. to Rt. standing:- Joan Hughes, Louise Doran, Joy Cooke, Barbara Parkes
Sitting: Elsie Jones, Norah Shields and Alice Deardon[UN]

Above: Members of the Pensioners' Club Bowls team, with a total age of 2,251 years and 1,309 years of Company service, about to set off for their annual match against Crosfields Pensioners at Warrington (the Port Sunlight team won by the narrow margin of eight points)[UN]

Above: *Thirty-five members of the newly-formed Motor Cycling Club pose outside the Main Offices before setting out on their excursion to Rhydymwyn, North Wales, in June 1949*[UNI]

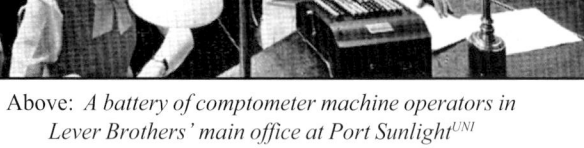

Above: *A battery of comptometer machine operators in Lever Brothers' main office at Port Sunlight*[UNI]

Right: *The carved stone Royal Coat of Arms above the entrance to the General offices, which was removed for safekeeping during the war, was re-erected in 1949 and has remained there ever since*

Left: *Winners of the 'Good Housekeeping' competition, the Tin-Plate Department from No3 Soapery about to set out on their expenses-paid trip to Blackpool in 1949*[UNI]

Jan 11 Memorial Stained-glass Window in Christ Church
Port Sunlight dedicated to Harold Robert
Greenhalgh, a director of Lever Bros for 25 years
and Vice-Chairman for 20 of those

Jan 25 Port Sunlight Gramophone Society formed -
it met in Hulme Hall – the aim of the society
was to emulate the spirit of the 'Proms' of the late
Sir Henry Wood

May 15 Field-Marshal the Viscount Montgomery of
Alamein, KG, CGB, DSO paid a visit to Port Sunlight,
and toured the factory and village (*see photo
opposite*)

May 27 Three-hole extension to Port Sunlight golf course
laid out on 8 acres of land on the other side of the
railway. This extended it as far as Spital Station, but
although re-shaped, it was still only 9 holes

Jun 7 On the eve of their first Test Match against England,
the West Indies Cricket Team visited Port Sunlight
(*see photos*)

Jul 22 The All England School Athletic Championship in
which over 1,400 young athletes took part was held
at the Port Sunlight Recreation Ground

Jul 28 Fountain outside Art Gallery 'Sea Piece' by Sir
Charles Wheeler RA switched on by the sculptor -
memorial to commemorate the birth of the first Lady
Lever 100 years ago (*see photo opposite*)

Aug Royal Warrant as 'Soap and Soap Powder
Manufacturers' to his Majesty the King was
renewed

Sep 10 Soap rationing ended

Oct The Oba of Benin (a state in Nigeria) with his eighth
and youngest wife, Ohan, and his son, Prince
Solomon, visited Port Sunlight – his country
produced palm oil and palm kernels which were
processed at Port Sunlight

Oct 1 Port Sunlight Hospital closed following introduction
of National Health Service

Nov 15 Former hospital re-opened as the Training Centre

Nov 20 The Olowo of Owo, Methodist ruler of 60,000
Nigerians, visited Port Sunlight

Nov 30 The Port Sunlight United Comrades' Federation's
new premises (in the refurbished Hesketh Hall) was
opened

Dec 1 The cast of *Rinso Roundabout*, the half-hour show
broadcast on Radio Luxembourg every Sunday
evening, visited Port Sunlight – they included Max
Wall, Deryck Guyler and Dorothy Summers (*see
photo*)

Dec 4 Port Sunlight Boys' Club new premises in Hesketh
Hall was officially opened

— Ownership of Oil & Cake Mills transferred to BEC
Ltd

— Productivity study and incentive scheme introduced
into Port

Above & Below: *The West Indies Cricket Team are seen visiting Port
Sunlight on the eve of their First Test Match against England. During
their tour they exclusively advertised* Rinso[UNI] *for washing their clothes*

Right: *Stars of the 'Rinso Radio Show' visit No.4 Soapery with Max
Wall crouching behind the* Rinso[UNI] *box looking at Hilda Robinson on
the packing line. The other stars were
Lt. to Rt.:- Mr H Cooper, Radio Productions Manager for Lintas;
Eric Whitley, 'the golden voice of* Rinso*'; Thea Wells, the* Rinso *housewife
was also 'the next door neighbour' in Mrs Dale's Diary;
Deryck ('Frisby Dyke') Guyler and Dorothy ('Mrs Mopp') Summers[UNI]*

Above: *Field-Marshal the Viscount Montgomery of Alamein, KG, CGB, DSO paid a visit to Port Sunlight on 15 May. He is seen here walking in front of the Mayor but he also travelled in an open Staff Car during his tour of the factory and village. The following year a new locomotive at Port Sunlight was named* Montgomery of Alamein *and was affectionately known as 'Monty'*[UNI]

Above: *Thousands of cardboard rolls waiting to be cut to length, fitted with their metal ends and filled with Vim*[UNI]

Right:
The crowning of the Carnival Queen, Hazel Woods, at the Port Sunlight Recreation Ground by the Mayoress of Bebington in front of 10,000 people[UNI]

Above: *The Port Sunlight Boys' Club team with their first major trophy the 'Russell Cup' which they won at the Boys' Club Championships in 1950. Lt. to Rt. Back row:- Bill Osborne, Leslie Dabbs, Eric Wardle, Henry Smith, Eddie Lamb, Tony Phillips, Don Blythe, Front row:- Norman Scott, Ray Burrows, Chris Gerrard, Mr JG McNeilly (warden), Brian Harris, Cyril Jones, and David Jones. Don Thomas was missing from the photograph*[UNI]

Above: *'Sea Piece', a sculpture in the form of a fountain by Sir Charles Wheeler RA was switched on in July 1950 by the sculptor outside the Lady Lever Art Gallery. Presented by the Trustees of the Gallery to Lever Brothers, it is actually a memorial commemorating the birth of the first Lady Lever 100 years ago*

Right: *For many years, employees were able to enter the factory from the New Chester Road across this narrow footbridge which spanned the River Dibbin near to its junction with Bromborough Pool. (Situated close to the existing vehicle entrance, it was eventually taken down in 1954 when this section of the river was culverted)*[UNI]

Below: On 21 December, Lord & Lady Leverhulme ceremonially named Port Sunlight's newest diesel locomotives Prince Charles and Princess Anne [UNI]

1951

Feb 28   Port Sunlight Boxing Club's first boxing tournament – held in the Men's Dining Hall

Mar   Alterations were made to the baths including: the wooden staging replaced by walls at each end of the pool; a foot-bath being provided and paving the grass verge behind the diving boards *(see photo 1952)*

Mar 10   At the Rugby Club Dinner, plans were revealed to replace the existing Recreation Ground (the Oval) with a new sports stadium on 100 acres of land at Bromborough between the New Chester Road and the Stork Margarine Works. The plans were originally drawn up in the 1930s but the war intervened. In the end the scheme was dropped and the land is now occupied by the Bromborough Retail Park. Leverhulme Playing Fields were later opened at Green Lane.

Apr 19   Princess Marie Louise (Queen Victoria's grand-daughter) visited works - she met 10 employees who had completed more than 50 years service

Apr 21   The Port Sunlight Recreation Ground at the Oval was the venue for the Ladies' Hockey International between England and Scotland – England won 4-2 in front of a 4,000 crowd

May   A new Unilever product is launched - *Breeze* - a quick lathering, mild green toilet soap for all the family *(see photo opposite)*

May 28   Miss Jean Kent, a glamorous British film star and a leading advertising figure for *Lux Soap* visited Port Sunlight and toured the factory

Jun 26   First of 10 Evening Cruises for employees aboard the new luxury ferry *Royal Iris (see photo opposite)*

Jul 24   The last of the 10 'Centenary' *Royal Iris* cruises in which over 7,000 employees and wives celebrated the birth 100 years ago of the first Viscount Leverhulme with a trip on the Mersey

Sep 15   New Mens' Club opened in the Lyceum

Sep 16   At the Centenary Service of the birth of the first Viscount Leverhulme, a commemorative tablet was unveiled to mark the restoration of the church bells

Sep 19   The Leverhulme Safety Trophy was presented by the 3rd Viscount Leverhulme to celebrate the Centenary of his Grandfather's birth

Above: An aerial view of Port Sunlight factory taken in the 1950s from the south-west. Centre left is the Printing Department with No.4 Soapery to its right. Bottom left are the loco sheds where the Company's fleet of locomotives was maintained

Right: A group of factory girls enjoying the 'Christening Ceremony' of the locomotives Prince Charles & Princess Ann (see below) [UNI]

1951

Sep 21/22   Two Centenary Balls were held in the replanned, refurbished and redecorated Hulme Hall

Sep 24   The Table Tennis Club moved to new quarters in the Assembly Rooms

Oct 4   *The Times* Festival of Britain Photographic Exhibition opened in Hulme Hall and was seen by some 1,500 people during the 6 days

Nov 30   The new Diesel-electric locomotive *Montgomery of Alamein* - used for haulage between 'Top Sidings' and Bromborough Power Station - was unveiled *(see photo opposite)*

Dec 21   Lord & Lady Leverhulme name the 2 new locomotives at Port Sunlight - *Prince Charles* and *Princess Anne (see photos)*

Dec   Port Sunlight's soap production reached an all-time record in 1951 of 195,000 tons

—   Port Sunlight AFC West Cheshire AF League Champions 1950/51 – 2nd Division Champions in the same year

—   Continuous system of soapmaking introduced at Port Sunlight

Above: Some of the employees and their wives who enjoyed one of the Royal Iris cruises in June 1951[UNI]

Left: An aerial view of the Port Sunlight factory from the north-west. In the centre the Oil & Cake Mills are alongside the Port Sunlight Dock. On the left the River Dibbin winds its way between steep banks towards Spital Dam

Right: Breeze Soap[UNI] was launched in April 1951. Manufactured at Port Sunlight but marketed by Lever Brothers' subsidiary Crosfields

Above: Accompanied by Mr George Nairn, Chairman of Lever Brothers, Lieut. Gen. Sir Cameron Nicholson GOC-in-C Western Command, officially named Port Sunlight's latest locomotive Montgomery of Alamein (affectionately known as 'Monty') on 30 November 1951[UNI]

Above: An aerial view of Port Sunlight from the west. The tall chimneys which dominated the factory were taken down in the 1950s when electricity and steam were no longer produced in the individual soaperies. The 'Top Sidings' can just be seen at the bottom right of the picture[UNI]

Jan 15 The Good Housekeeping Award went to the Girls'
         Cafeteria
Jan 22 The Apprentices' Training Workshop, in the former
         Gas Decontamination building in Lodge Lane,
         opened by the Chairman of Lever Brothers &
         Unilever Limited - Sir Geoffrey Heyworth [now
         demolished and Philip Leverhulme Lodge built on
         the site]
Feb 5   The Board of Lever Brothers & Unilever Limited
         announced that, at an EGM on 27 February, a
         Special Resolution would be submitted to change
         the name to Unilever Limited. The name Lever
         Brothers would still be retained in the UK in the title
         of the marketing company and as the manufacturing
         company of Lever Brothers, Port Sunlight
Feb 6   **King George VI died**
Mar 29 Eight Port Sunlight boys were chosen from a variety
         of departments to take part in the Outward Bound
         Schools venture at Aberdovey or Eskdale
Apr   The Wharf at Port Sunlight underwent a
         transformation when most of the old cast-iron and
         steelwork wharf was encased in concrete
         (*see photo*)
Sep 2   Launch of *Surf* (manufactured at Warrington)
Oct   *Lifebuoy Soap* and *Sunlight Soap* both underwent
         a packaging update with newly designed packs
         which had changed from a carton to a streamlined
         wrapper produced from lacquered paper (*see
         photos*)

Above: *Some of Port Sunlight's Estates Department gardeners who
were responsible for the lawns and flowerbeds in the village, as well as
seven soccer pitches, two rugby grounds, 11 tennis courts, three cricket
pitches and three hockey pitches at the Oval Recreation Ground. From
Rt. to Lt.: Duncan Menzies, Sam Parry, Sep Ellison and Arthur
Willis*[UNI]

*During, and after the war, restrictions had meant that soap was sold
without any wrapping. In 1952 a new wrapper was introduced for*
Lifebuoy[UNI] *and* Sunlight,[UNI] *both are seen here*

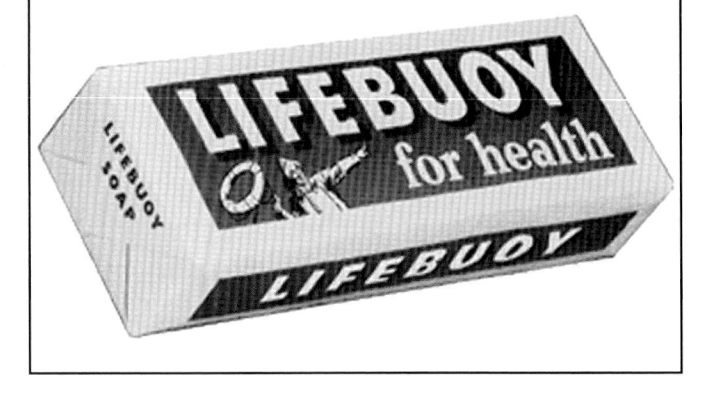

Above: *A group of sailors from the US Navy who spent the day in
Port Sunlight on 18 March 1952*[UNI]

Above: *Port Sunlight's 1st XI Cricket Team*
*Lt. to Rt. Back row: AF Barker (umpire), B Kilburn (Club Secretary),
KJ Parsons, RI Rowland, E Richards, R Williamson, E Molyneux
Front row: CG Davies, EV Pugh (Vice Captain), J Bewley (Captain),
J Dobson, K Green, E Pritchard (Scorer)*[UNI]

Above: *The barges* Elizabeth *and* Lobol *are seen here tied up at the
Port Sunlight Wharf after its reconstruction in 1952*[UNI]

Right & Below: *These two pictures of Port Sunlight Wharf were taken at the same time, but from slightly different angles. The tall tower marks the spot where work on Port Sunlight ceremonially began on 3 March 1888. On the right of the upper picture are the 'timber sheds' where wood for making the wooden soap boxes was stored. The wharves, seen here after reconstruction in 1952, were connected by an underground conveyor tunnel to the No.1 factory. This enabled the soap cases to be moved directly to the lower wharf for loading onto barges*

Below: *The engine* Alberta *is seen here on the top sidings at Port Sunlight. Built in 1913, it was finally sold in 1956*

Below: *The Engraving Shop where skilled craftsmen produced all the intricate 'dies' used to manufacture the various soap tablets in the Port Sunlight factory*[UNI]

Above: *Although this postcard was sent in 1952 the photograph was presumably taken before the alterations of March 1951 to the open-air baths, when the walls at each end of the bath replaced the wooden staging, the grass verge behind the diving board was paved over and a foot-bath provided*

Feb   Following floods at their Purfleet factory, the Stork Margarine Works of Van den Berghs and Jurgens ceased production there. This was made good by the Bromborough Works achieving a 100% increase in margarine output by 'working round the clock'

Mar 1   No.5 Soapery opened to produce NSD (Non Soap Detergent) washing powders

Jun   Centenary Celebration of the abolition of the Soap Tax - Mr CA Gladstone DL, JP, unveiled a new hanging sign outside Gladstone Hall which was named after his grandfather and depicted the Gladstone Coat of Arms (*see photo*)

Jun 2   **Queen Elizabeth II's Coronation Day**
        During the Coronation period, the office buildings and houses in Port Sunlight Village were hung with banners, bunting, pennants and shields (*see photo opposite* – there were children's parties arranged, a Coronation Service in Christ Church, a Coronation Exhibition on the ground floor of the Library, and 3 Coronation Dances held in Hulme Hall, as well as other celebrations

Jun 14 Sixty-six Port Sunlight people visited Holland at the invitation of Unilever's Dutch Management

Sep 11 Port Sunlight Golf Club moved to new clubhouse in the former nutrition laboratory (*see photo*)

Sep 18 New Diesel Locomotives *Lord Leverhulme* and *Lady Leverhulme* named at a ceremony at Port Sunlight

"Have you any LIFEBUOY?"

"Just try me girlie, JUST TRY ME!"

Above: *A soap comic postcard of the 1950s*[UNI]

Right: *This postcard shows the original Stork Margarine Offices on Stadium Road in the 1950s. The grand columns which grace the front of the building came from the bandstand in Port Sunlight (*see 1932*), made of timber they were later burnt after the building was demolished*

Left: *To commemorate the centenary of the abolition of the 'Soap Tax', a new sign depicting the Gladstone Coat of Arms was unveiled in June by Mr CA Gladstone, grandson of Prime Minister William Gladstone who originally opened the Hall in 1891*

Right:
On 11 September 1953, the former 'Nutrition Laboratory' was re-opened by Mr GAS Nairn, Chairman of Lever Brothers, as the new club house for the Port Sunlight Golf Club[UNI]

'... and so comes to an end the first sixty-five years in the life of Port Sunlight. Sixty-five years that saw green fields develop into a thriving industrial complex and village community. A community that lived through two world wars and saw six monarchs on the throne, starting and ending with a queen. A community that lived, worked and played together through an age of radical changes, changes that still continue today. Fifty years on, we can still look back at its traditions, preserved in its buildings, its societies, its people and not least through the images that remind us of what life was like in

Above: In 1953 many people still came to work by bus, and the dozens of buses waiting outside the Port Sunlight factory were a familiar sight with queues of employees waiting behind the barriers introduced in 1949 UNI

Above: A view of the Bowling Green and Silver Wedding Fountain in its current position, with the General Offices beyond, the District Bank on the left and the Lever Library next door

Below: Lever Brothers' main office buildings can be seen adorned with banners, bunting and shields to celebrate the Coronation of Queen Elizabeth II

Right: The train is pictured at Port Sunlight Station having transported employees from Chester and other stations along the line UNI

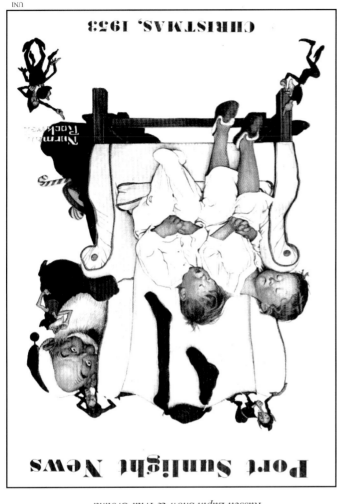

Port Sunlight News

CHRISTMAS, 1953

Above: Members of the Port Sunlight Allotment Holders' Society on an outing in 1953 to the Bromingdale Nurseries, home of the famou Russell Lupin Show & Trial Ground UNI

Port Sunlight's Photographer
J George Davies

Port Sunlight must rank high amongst any claims to be the most photographed village in the country. From the very beginning, events were recorded by both national and local photographers, and in particular, throughout its history postcards have provided an invaluable pictorial record of the factory and village. Right from the beginning, Lever Brothers had their own photographers, but only two of their names are mentioned in any early publications about Port Sunlight. Originally attached to the Printing Department, they were both called George - Jonathon George Davies, or as he is better known, George Davies, and George Cotton. Whilst some of the early pictures in this book were taken by George Cotton, a vast number from the early part of the twentieth century are the work of George Davies.

George Cotton was the son of a Liverpool printer. Originally a litho printer, George was the Company's first official photographer and spent the rest of his career as a photographer with the Company until his retirement in the 1930s. George Davies, the better known of the two was the son of William Hesketh Lever's coachman, who was also called George Davies. The young George apparently spent his childhood in and around Lever's home at Thornton Manor where his father worked, but unlike his namesake, young George didn't stay with the Company. Instead he left and went into business for himself as a photographer and producer of postcards.

At the beginning he was working from his home on Corniche Road in Port Sunlight village. Then from his house right alongside the bridge which carried the New Chester Road over Bromborough Pool. Before the widespread use of telephones, postcards were a very efficient way of sending messages. In 1907, when George Davies opened his first shop on Bebington Road, some 800 million postcards were posted in the UK alone. As the business grew, so George moved into new premises; first into a shop on the New Chester Road in New Ferry where a supermarket stands today, and then into purpose built premises on the corner of Beaconsfield Road and New Chester Road opposite Hesketh Hall.

Although he had his own business, much of his work was still for Lever Brothers and for Mr Lever himself – often photographing events at Mr & Mrs Lever's home at Bolton, as well as the various festivities at Thornton Manor. Many of George Davies' pictures of Port Sunlight are characterised by the inclusion of his family at various staged in their development, whilst those taken elsewhere in Wirral feature his bicycle. He also seems to have travelled extensively around the north west on his motorcycle taking photographs to illustrate his postcards, and in the latter years he had a cottage on the Horseshoe Pass near Llangollen.

In 1914 George Davies turned part of the ground floor of his shop into New Ferry's first labour exchange. During the Great War he served in the 'Worcesters' and was wounded and captured in May 1918, spending his 40th birthday as a prisoner of war. When he returned home after the war he seems to have almost given up being a photographer to concentrate on running the labour exchange, which is how his family remember him. His parents retired to live in Windy Bank in Port Sunlight where his father died in 1947 at the age of 88. George himself died in 1951, and the shop passed to the Hemmings brothers who ran a photographic business there for many years, later to be succeeded by CJ Studios.

Together with his parents, his wife Margaretta, and his son Alan, George Davies is buried at Christ Church in Port Sunlight village – the village that he spent so much of his early life photographing and recording for posterity.

Left: *George Davies with his family. Lt. to Rt. Standing: Winnie, Bill, Nancy, Jean, Bob, & Doris. Seated: George, Alan, & Margaretta*

J. Geo. Davies,
PHOTOGRAPHER,
The Studio, New Ferry.
OPPOSITE TECHNICAL INSTITUTE

Photographs in all the latest Styles, Artistic Lighting and Mounting.

Wedding groups a Speciality.   Moderate Charges.

Above: *An advertisement for George Davies' business on the corner of the New Chester Road and Beaconsfield Road, (see opposite)*

Index

Left: *Photographed by George Davies,
his shop on the corner of Beaconsfield
Road is seen here bedecked with bunting
for the Royal Visit on 25 March 1914*

Below: *This photograph of Hulme
Hall, which was taken by George
Davies in the early 1900s, includes
three of his children, who appeared
regularly in his picture postcards*

117